13732

The Magic and Mystery

of Words

Books by J. Donald Adams

The Shape of Books to Come
Literary Frontiers
Copey of Harvard:
A Biography of Charles Townsend Copeland

Edited by J. Donald Adams

The Treasure Chest:
An Anthology of Contemplative Prose

The New Treasure Chest:
An Anthology of Reflective Prose

Triumph Over Odds:
An Anthology of Man's Unconquerable Spirit

T H E

Magic and Mystery

O F

Words

By J. Donald Adams

Holt, Rinehart and Winston

NEW YORK   CHICAGO   SAN FRANCISCO

To the memory

of

Charles Townsend Copeland,

who taught me what words

can do.

Foreword

THIS BOOK makes no pretension to authority. As a writer, I am a professional user of words, but I lay no claim to linguistic scholarship, and make no effort here to prove or disprove the theories that have been advanced regarding the origin and development of language. To be sure, I may sometimes state a preference for a certain point of view, for what this book does is to record my reactions, as you might record yours, to the miracle of speech—the power to express himself that has made possible the extraordinary history of man. If it were not for this gift of communication, beginning with the grunts and ejaculations of his remote ancestors, and flowering into the manifold media, written and otherwise, which we now possess, his history would be as blank as that of the lower primates.

What follows is an informal account of the fascination I find in words, of my likes and dislikes among them, with some speculation as to their nature and history. In them are reflected all the delights and miseries of human existence.

My thanks are due to the many writers on the subject of words whose thoughts have stimulated my own. I am indebted to the New York *Times* for permission to include certain passages from my Sunday column, "Speaking of Books"; to Houghton Mifflin Company for a passage from George R. Stewart's *Names on the Land;* to Alfred A. Knopf, Inc., for several quotations from Walter de la Mare's *Come Hither;* to E. P. Dutton & Co. for the inclusion of others from the introductions I wrote for the word anthologies of Ivor Brown; and to Duell, Sloan & Pearce for permission to use part of the chapter on words in *Literary Frontiers.* Much the greater part of this book, however, has not heretofore appeared in print.

—J. D. A.

Contents

The Magic and Mystery

of Words

I

What Words Are

HAS IT ever occurred to you how much words have in common with money? They are first of all counters of exchange; they are sometimes inflated and frequently devalued, put in circulation and withdrawn. They, too, accumulate interest, they are coined, they are borrowed, they grow blurred with use, they are hoarded and they are spent lavishly. They can be counterfeit. They convince and they seduce. They are accepted (too often) at face value, and they lend themselves easily to speculation, or I would not be writing these particular words.

As a subject for comment, words are almost on a par with the weather in their universality of appeal. We all use them, poorly or well, and for good or ill; we all have some interest in them, if it is only in the solving of crossword puzzles. Books about them multiply; newspapers run prize contests based on their use; magazines prod us into enlarging our vocabularies. Is it paradoxical that so much attention should be paid them at a time when they are more carelessly used and more rapidly debased than ever before, or is this increased attention the result of their abuse?

In either case, the situation is strange. Surely there was never a time in which so many different groups of people— including hipsters, horseplayers, sportswriters, sociologists, gossip columnists, psychoanalysts, educators, mobsters, fashion experts, hucksters, physicists and technologists, bureaucrats and teen-agers—have insisted on divorcing themselves from the common tongue and developing a distinctive lingo. At the present rate of acceleration the time cannot be distant when, in the interest of easier communication, we shall have to devise a new *lingua franca*. Perhaps it would be simpler to take over the old sign language which served the Plains Indians so well.

Whatever the present situation, words remain one of the most living things of man's creation; indeed, one might argue that they have more vitality than anything else we have fashioned. What else is there that seems to lead an independent life? Words do; they acquire strength and lose it; they may, like people, become transformed in character; like certain persons, they may gather evil about them, or like others, prod our wits or lift our hearts. Like ourselves, some of them suffer from hardening of the arteries. They seem to pursue their own ends with a dogged intention, and when, utterly spent and cast out from the common tongue, they fall into obsolescence, not all the lexicographers and etymologists together can revive them.

4

During wars and immediately after them, words—particularly those that stand for big and ideal concepts—are likely to have a hollow sound and to grow fuzzy and frayed at the edges, if not somewhat rotten at the heart. Except in their most simple and direct uses, they are not much good in time of war, though we are then pelted with them even more than we are in the intervals of peace. However much we may talk about them as weapons—which they can be—when armies are on the march and the earth shakes, words assume a triviality which belies their true nature. They have a lot to do with making wars, but save for those we speak of as cold, not much with winning them.

Our greatly increased interest in semantics, the science of meanings, is not, I think, a merely chance matter. Words are more important today than ever before, because men have become less united in their attitudes, and have increasing difficulty in understanding one another. Words were less important in the Middle Ages, when people were sustained by a deeply felt religious faith that permeated their lives and when all values were more clearly defined and more universally shared. Even as recently as the nineteenth century Western man, at least, firmly believed in continual progress and the perfectibility of man. Our divisions today are found in more intangible barriers than those of the Berlin wall and the Iron Curtain. As Albert Camus observed, it would seem now as if "man's long dialogue" had come to an end. I said earlier that words have much in common with money, but there is a great difference too, in that they are living tissue, sensitive organisms that require the most careful handling. When casually shoved in the slot like tokens on a bus, or used, as they so often are in an age of universal and insistent propaganda, to act like the inky effluvia of the squid, they become obscuring and destructive forces of great potency.

Man's other creations all require a material embodiment of some kind. Words stand alone. Although they appear in type or on the phonograph disk, they are not dependent on them as architecture is dependent upon steel and stone, wood and glass; or painting upon colors and canvas; or sculpture upon marble or bronze; music on its instruments or practical science on its technological embodiments. Words alone are as disembodied as when man first drew them from his stream of thought. Though they are transmitted by his vocal cords, by the gestures of his hands, or by the medium of print, they are capable of free existence in his brain, like a wish, an ambition, a love. They had to exist there before he could utter them, or by sign communicate their meaning.

Nothing in man's development from the so-called lower orders seems to me as fascinating, as teasing to the mind, as the process by which he developed the capacity for speech. All of us who use words, whether as tools in our work or merely as the means of day-to-day communication with our fellows, must sometimes pause to ponder over their beginnings and to wonder at the frequently brilliant suggestiveness of the symbols chosen by those remote ancestors who looked with fresh eyes upon the phenomena of nature and sought to find, in speech, sounds that would convey what they saw. For all the theories that have been spun about the origins of language, we know with certainty very little about them. All is conjecture, all is shrouded in the mists of an age of which our only records lie in the rocks, or in the forms of animal and vegetable life—and these records, however much else they may tell us, have nothing to say of speech. The question of its origin is the more teasing because the likelihood of our ever learning any more than we now know is small indeed.

Our ignorance about how language began is much like

our ignorance of the history of man's knowledge of what things in nature were suitable for him to eat and of what things he could use to cure his ills. There, too, we are stranded on islands of conjecture. All we truly know is that man, beyond all other forms of animal life, was endowed with intelligent and reasoning curiosity, with a daring, deep-seated compulsion toward adventure, which should leave us speechless with self-admiration. I like to think of those bold experimenters, so many of whom must have surrendered their lives in the quest for this kind of knowledge. Think of those early men who stumbled upon the properties of herbs, the ones that stimulate the heart and those that depress it; the samplers of deadly poisons of which they knew nothing until they swallowed them; think of that man who, in the classic example, pried open an oyster for the first time, and ate it; the first finders and eaters of mushrooms and toad-stools in the forest, the deadly and the nutritious. Man's eating of the flesh of other animals was, of course, instinctive, since he is by nature carnivorous, but the range of his contemporary diet is evidence of his curiosity and courage. What an absorbing history it would make could it be written!

So it is with the history of language. How we would like to know! Did the old man of the tribe say we will call this thing that, and give it a name? Was there a council, and were other suggestions offered? There are too many obviously echoic words, words that attempt to approximate in sound the things for which they stand, for us not to believe that there sometimes was a conscious effort toward duplication in speech of what had been observed or heard in experience. To use what is for me an enticing example, consider the ancient Greek word for the sea, which was *thalassa*. To my ear, it conveys the sound of water slapping against a rock or the side of a boat. It is easy to carry these things too far, and I know that the scientific students of language are mistrustful of many so-called echoic words. Yet, knowing as little as we do, can we not make guesses?

I shall have more to say about echoic words, but in connection with the power of specific words to evoke the physical phenomena of which they are the symbols, let us consider for a moment some which do not achieve their effect by imitating certain sounds, but which nevertheless seem admirably suited to call up the image of what they are meant to stand for. There are two old English words which have come down unsullied through the centuries, unchanged in their pronunciation and in their meaning, and which have long seemed to me singularly figurative. They represent two of earth's universal and persistently repeated phenomena: dawn and dusk. I have always taken pleasure in both the sight and sound of these words. To me, there is slowly spreading light in the word *dawn,* both to the eye as we see it in print, and to the ear as we hear it spoken. So far as the eye is concerned, this effect is partly due, I think, to the fact that "a" is a bright letter; it lets in light. For that reason I prefer the spelling "grey" to "gray," because the first seems to me more shadowed. And when we hear the sound that *dawn* makes, surely the lengthiness and opening out of that single syllable suggest the gradual filling of the sky with light. *Daybreak* is a good word, too, but it carries with it a sense of abruptness which we do not associate with what actually happens when night gives place to day, even if Kipling wrote that "the dawn comes up like thunder."

Similarly, when we hear the word *dusk,* there is about the sound of it a suggestion of stealthiness, of the creeping up of night. Old as they are, unspoiled as they are, these two

8

words are more commonly used in writing than in speech. No words could be simpler or more expressive, but in ordinary speech we are more likely to use *sunrise* and *twilight*, or, in certain localities of the United States, *sunup* and *sundown*. Is it because of the beauty of *dawn* and *dusk* that they have acquired a somewhat literary character, so that we are a trifle self-conscious about their casual use? Certainly they are still fresh and unstained; yet *dawn* comes down to us from the Anglo-Saxon verb *dagian,* which in Middle English became *dawnen,* and *dusk* from the Anglo-Saxon *dosc* and the Middle English *dosk* or *dusk*. Fifteen centuries have failed to stale them.

This book is concerned chiefly with the magic and the mystery of words, and in this introductory chapter I wish to suggest how strongly they are endowed with those two qualities. It is interesting to note how much the effect of certain words upon us can be altered by a slight change in them, and how a certain phrase can be undermined by the substitution of one word for another of almost but not quite equivalent meaning. In *The Summing Up,* although Somerset Maugham contends that the language of the King James version has had a deleterious effect upon subsequent English prose, he refers to its *majestical* quality. Normally I prefer a short word to a longer one, but it seems to me that in this instance *majestical* adds a measure of weight where it is needed that *majestic* does not have.

In the matter of phrases in which slight alteration has disproportionate effect, suppose we consider the Biblical phrase "beside the still waters." *Quiet* is a synonym for *still,* but if it is substituted for the word chosen by the King James translators, the magic of the phrase is for me impaired. *Still* seems to me a quieter word than *quiet,* which is actually

9

rather noisy. *Still* is like dropping a pebble in an unruffled pool, and watching the circles silently widening out. With *quiet* you have just the plop of the pebble.

Nothing truer was ever said about the essential nature of words than was spoken by Elihu Root half a century ago, when he was arguing the Atlantic Fisheries case before the Supreme Court. "Words," he said, "are like those insects that take their color from their surroundings. Half the mis-understanding in this world comes from the fact that the words that are spoken or written are conditioned in the mind that gives them forth by one set of thoughts and ideas, and they are conditioned in the mind of the hearer or reader by another set of thoughts and ideas, and even the simplest forms of expression are frequently quite open to mistake, unless the hearer or reader can get some idea of what were the conditions in the brain from which the words come."

I suspect that one of the first steps necessary to getting ourselves and the world out of the mess we are in, is to be-come clear in our minds as to just what we mean by certain words, and also what other people mean, who use them in what may seem to us a quite different sense. I am thinking, of course, of words like *democracy, liberal,* and *conservative.* George Orwell may have hit on a profound truth when he assumed that the present political chaos is connected with the decay of language, and that some improvement might be brought about by starting at the verbal level.

There is much more to this situation, however, than the loose or inappropriate use of words arising out of careless-ness or ignorance. Orwell called attention to the fact that in our time a good part of political speech and writing is de-voted, through a carefully disingenuous use of words, to "the defense of the indefensible." He had particular reference to the dishonest nice Nellieness with which some of the characteristic deviltries of our era are described. The bombardment of defenseless villages has too often gone by the deceptively innocent term, *pacification.* Or when millions of peasants are robbed of their farms and sent trudging along the roads with no more than they can carry, such whitewashing phrases are used as "transfer of population" or "rectification of frontiers." When men are sent to prison without trial, or bundled off to concentration camps, phrases like "elimination of unreliable elements" are called into use. In this fashion it is possible to name horrible things without creating mental pictures of them. Such is the power of words.

Orwell hazarded the guess that the German, Italian, and Russian languages all deteriorated as a result of the word jockeying that ensued as soon as dictatorship in one form or another fastened itself upon these peoples. It seems a reasonable assumption, because even in Great Britain and the United States the growth of bureaucracy, if not comparable to that in the totalitarian states, has nevertheless been sufficient to make clearly perceptible some weakening in the fiber of English. There has been an increase of muddiness, clumsiness, and circumlocution, and the changes have been definitely on the side of deception and concealment. We like to think of ours as a time when plain speaking and writing are better appreciated than they were in some periods of the past; we are proud of the fact that Fourth of July oratory now sounds hollow in our ears, and we boast of our readiness to call a spade a spade, but we are guilty of some strange contradictions of that attitude.

Language being the responsive medium it is, one deeply affected by the temper and attitudes of the period to which it belongs, it is only natural that the way in which words are used in our time should reflect our confusion and our awareness of shifting values. But language is not only acted *upon*—it is an active force itself, capable of affecting our attitudes and ideas; and that is why we must give increasing thought to words and to the power within them.

I took as a title for this introductory chapter, "What Words Are." "Uttering a word," wrote Ludwig Wittgenstein, "is like striking a note on the keyboard of the imagination." And Emerson said, "Every word was once a poem." A few of them, I think, still are. Surely that may be said of such words as *dawn* and *dusk,* whose poetry lies in their suggestiveness. It is also true of some place-names, whose beauty is solely that of sound, like Susquehanna and Shenandoah. Words, then, are like money, counters of exchange; they are living entities; they were, and sometimes still are, poems; they are persuaders and fortifiers, tranquilizers and irritants; and they are forces for good or evil—builders and destroyers. Suppose we now pursue a little further the question of their origin, of how they came to be.

I I

The Dawn of Language

THE OLDEST and simplest theory of the origin of language is contained in two sentences from Genesis: "And out of the ground the Lord God formed every beast of the field, and every fowl of the air; and brought them unto Adam to see what he would call them: and whatsoever Adam called every creature, that was the name thereof. And Adam gave names to all cattle, and to the fowl of the air, and to every beast of the field. . . ." Today we regard this as a naïve and insufficient explanation, such a one as any primitive people might devise for itself. Yet it does rest on a basis of truth. Man *did* name the animals, but we now suspect that there was a long progress in speech before he was able to do what the author or authors of Genesis ascribed to Adam.

Our only definite knowledge about the evolution of language dates from the time when man began to put down, first by carving on stone, then in writing, the words he had already been using—for how long we are not sure. It has been estimated that at least eighty thousand years have elapsed since true speech began, and what is known about the speech habits of man is confined to only about four thousand. Of the period between the time when man became articulate—with the first grunts or exclamations—and the time of the first inscriptions, we can speak with no confidence whatever. All is conjecture.

Yet it is conjecture that is extraordinarily teasing to the mind, or, more specifically, to the imagination. Linguistic scholars have written long treatises on the subject, and they have constructed ingenious and sometimes plausible theories. Beginning with Socrates, as recorded in the *Cratylus* of Plato, many men have attempted more searching and more elaborate explanations than the simple, forthright, childlike one that we find in Genesis. None, however, has as yet been universally accepted, as we now accept, for example, established scientific theory concerning the origin of animal life. Only a year or so ago a new theory was advanced by Dr. A. S. Diamant, an English lawyer and sociologist. He undertook to prove that the first words were brief exclamations— little more than gasps—and not unlike the first articulate utterances of babies. They came, he thinks, out of the need for action, and were a call for assistance from one man to another. The sounds were accompanied by a strenuous effort of the arm, in a gesture intended to illustrate the kind of assistance needed—usually to cut, break, strike, or crush something.

Such an explanation may seem like pure conjecture, yet Dr. Diamant bases his conclusions on an impressive array of data drawn from human physiology, the first attempts at speech by children, animal behavior, and finally, the evidence surviving in some of the oldest languages, such as Hebrew and Bantu, which, in spite of their age, have changed less than others. The process by which he arrived at these conclusions is too complex for exposition here.

Among the theories which have preceded his, the best-known is probably the onomatopoeic, which finds the origin of speech in the imitation of natural sounds. Max Mueller, one of the numerous German scholars who have delved in these mysteries, christened this the bow-wow theory. It is first found in the talk of Socrates, as set down by Plato, and as we shall see, he had some cogent reasons for his belief. Today a majority of linguistic scientists regard it as affording only a partial explanation of the development of language. Aristotle, incidentally, would have none of the idea of the natural fitness of words to signify meaning. He foreshadowed the doctrine that the meaning of words is derived from their use.

Then there is the theory that language originated in those cries of the human animal which are approximated by the lower orders. But they, it is argued, are solely the expression of emotion, whereas in what may properly be called language, however primitive, there is something, however slight, of intellectual content. It is difficult to see how one could develop from the other—that is, how mere exclamations of emotion could evolve into conceptual statements—since the difference between them is one of kind and not of degree.

Still another theory found the source of speech in acts of common or joint work, like pulling on a rope or dragging a tree. This is close to Dr. Diamant's theory, but he could find no trace, in the ancient languages he examined, of a single original root signifying to pull or drag. It has also been argued that language originated in gesture, to which the objection can be made that a gesture cannot become a word or sentence. The strangest theory of all, perhaps, was that advanced by the Danish scholar, Otto Jesperson, who maintained that speech began as song, composed of very long words. This he based largely on the existence of our tendency to shorten words and to make pronunciation of them easier. But, as Dr. Diamant points out, there is also a tendency to lengthen words, which shows itself in English in the development of that language from the Anglo-Saxon.

It is possible, of course, to draw certain deductions regarding the character of speech when words first began to be used. Frederick Bodmer, in *The Loom of Language* has, for example, drawn up a classification of the elements of language appropriate to a primitive level of human communication. His guess is that they comprised "substantives, or individual words used for distinct objects or events which can be indicated by pointing at things—such as our words *dog* or *thunder*"; and then, at a later stage, came words indicating certain qualities, such as *red* or *noisy*. Then came another group, composed of vocatives, "short signals used to call forth some response, such as our words *where? stop, run, come pull!* and names of individuals." A third group would be made up of "demonstratives, or gesture substitutes which direct the attention of the listener to a particular point in a situation, *i.e., that, here, behind, in front*." Finally, there would be "incorporatives, or recitative combinations of sound used in ritual incantations without any recognition of separate elements corresponding to what we would call *words*."

Let us now go back for a moment to Socrates and Plato. In the course of the dialogue, Socrates observed the frequency with which the letter "r" appears in words expressing motion; this, we may note, is true not only of the Greek, but of English as well: *run, river, ripple, rise, race, ride, rattle,* etc. He also observed how the letter "l" expresses smoothness, as in the Greek word for which the English equivalent is *level*. Such instances led him to offer the theory that "the correct name indicates the nature of the thing." And, of course, even those who will not accept the Socratic theory of onomatopoeia in toto, have to admit that a great many words are obviously echoic, or imitative of what they represent. Words like *splash* and *thump* come readily to mind. A particularly striking example is provided by the word *thunder,* because its plainly echoic character is evident in the equivalent words in several other languages, as *tonnerre* in French, *grom* in Russian, and *donner* in German.

It is hard to rid ourselves of the idea that the desire to name things lies at the root of language. It is almost instinctual for anyone learning a new language to ask what certain objects are called; that is almost invariably the first step we take. In George R. Stewart's *Names on the Land,* which is chiefly concerned with place-naming in the United States, he offers a vivid re-creation of what probably happened when primitive man first set about making himself feel more at home in his environment by naming certain aspects, certain landmarks he wished to remember:

Once, let us say, some tribesmen moved toward a new country, which was unknown to them. Halting, they chose a good man, and sent him ahead. This scout went on, watching not to be ambushed or get lost, knowing he must report shrewdly when he returned. First he skulked along the edge of a big meadow, where he saw many deer. Then he came to a stream where he noted some oak trees, which were uncommon in that country. All this time he was skirting the slope of a great mountain, but because he was actually on it, and because the trees were so thick, he did not think of a mountain; and besides, it made no difference to him one way or the other. So he went farther on—through a little swamp, and to a stream which he crossed on a beaver-dam. The stream was the same as the one where the oak trees grew, but he had no way of being certain, and besides it did not matter at all— each crossing was a thing in itself. He went on, through a narrow defile with many tall rocks, which he knew would be an ugly spot for an ambush. Going back, he noted all the places in reverse, but did not actually bestow any names on them.

When he told his story, however, he unconsciously gave names by describing places, such as the big meadow and the stream where the oak trees grew. He did not speak of the mountain, because the mountain was everywhere and the whole country was merely its slope; and he did not speak of the deer in the meadow, because he knew that deer are at one place for sun-up and another for nooning, so that only a fool would try to distinguish one meadow from another by mentioning them.

The others listened to his words, nodded and questioned and remembered; they knew that they would have no other knowledge of the next day's march, and that life and death might hang on how well they remembered his landmarks. So they thought to themselves, "big meadow," "stream where oak trees grow," "stream with a beaver-dam," and the rest. When they went ahead into that country, they recognized each place as they came to it.

Then, when they lived there, they used the descriptions first, saying, "There is good fishing in the stream where oak trees grow." But soon they said, "stream-where-oak-trees-grow" in one breath, and it had become a name.

The first simple names were like sign-posts, noting something permanent and easily recognized, something to distinguish one place from other places—size, or shape, or color, or the kind of rocks or trees found there. After the tribe grew familiar with the region, such sign-post names were no longer much needed, and as the people began to have memories of what had happened there, names of another kind sprang up.

At some stream, perhaps, a hunter saw a panther drinking in broad daylight, and killed it with a single arrow. This was a matter of wonder, and people began to say: "the stream where the panther was killed." After a few generations the actual story may have been forgotten, but the name retained. In the old Choctaw country there is still a Quilly Creek, from their words *koi-ai-albi*, "panther-there-killed." Far in the Southwest a ruined pueblo is Callemongue, "where-they-hurled-down-stones." But the name is the only testimony; no man knows the story of that desperate siege, or who hurled down stones at what besiegers.

It is likely that gesture preceded speech, which it has always accompanied, for gesture is instinctual—as much so as the dog's wagging of his tail or the cat's arching of her back. In moments of stress or strong emotion, we are all likely to resort to it: a gesture of fear, resolution, anger, or delight. Some nationalities are more prone to its use than others; an Italian or a Frenchman finds it difficult to express himself without the aid of his hands, whereas a Scot or an Englishman, let us say, regards gesture as waste effort. At least, he is manually less demonstrative.

A few pages back I suggested, not too seriously, that, in view of the current multiplication of private languages among special groups, we might do well to resort to the use of Indian sign. Its origin is interesting. Nothing in the history of the North American Indian is more noteworthy than the extraordinary diversification of language among the tribes that peopled this continent. It was Thomas Jefferson, in his *Notes on the State of Virginia,* who observed that for one "radical language" in Asia there would probably be found twenty in America, and he himself collected and arranged the vocabularies of some fifty Indian languages and dialects. His Secretary of the Treasury, Albert Gallatin, carried on further studies in this field, as did, much later, Major J. R. Powell and Dr. D. G. Brinton. Powell determined that there were no less than fifty-eight distinct linguistic stocks of American Indians north of Mexico. Indian sign developed—just when we do not know—because even adjacent tribes of the same ethnic group were unable to communicate with one another verbally.

The number of living Indians skillful in the use of sign is rapidly diminishing. Its use is now confined almost wholly to the old men—the "long-braids"—and the men have always used it, understandably perhaps, more than the women. Very few of the young people in any of the Plains tribes trouble to learn it, and the chances are that before this century is ended Indian sign will be as dead a language as Latin or ancient Greek. And that will be a pity, because, in expert use, it is a subtle and beautiful form of communication. Several years ago, while visiting on the reserve of the Canadian Bloods (a branch of the Blackfeet), in the Province of Alberta, I was taught its rudiments by an old Assiniboin named Charlie Bear, a visitor at the Sun Dance of the Bloods, who are, incidentally, more completely full-blooded than any Plains tribe still existent in North America. Seeing them, you see the Plains Indian much as he was in the days of the buffalo—and a fine-looking breed of men they are.

Indian sign, as practiced by those who know it well, is fascinating to watch, even to one who knows nothing of it. It has a flow, a grace, which are absent from its nearest equivalent, the sign language used by the deaf and dumb. Also it often has an element of poetry less present in the latter. When, for example, an Indian, talking sign, wishes you to know that he is feeling sad, he places his right hand over his heart, and then, with a flowing movement, lets his open palm sweep slowly toward the ground. Many words are imaginatively expressed. In signing *day,* the speaker holds his hands level, backs up, in front of his face, about four inches apart, then sweeps them up and out in a curve, ending opposite his shoulders, with the palms now up. And *night* (which would mean to the Indian, earth covered over), he would express by extending flat hands in front of him, ten inches apart, with the backs up, and the right hand a little higher than the left; then he would move his right hand to the left and the left to the right, turning his hands slightly by action of his wrists.

One drawback of sign, of course, is that in darkness communication is difficult or impossible. But what a boon it would be for use at cocktail parties, at political conventions, or at the theater! Mastering it, we could alleviate a few of the minor tensions and irritants of urban life.

III

Beauty in Words

I HAVE SAID little about the beauty that words can convey. More of that later; just now I would like to consider such beauty as they may be said to have in themselves, out of context. Do individual words have an esthetic quality that is pleasing to the eye or ear, or to both? It is an arguable question, though I believe the weight of evidence is in the affirmative.

T. S. Eliot is one of those who incline to the negative. In his essay, "The Music of Poetry," he says, "I doubt whether, from the point of view of *sound* alone, any word is more or less beautiful than another—within its own language, for the question whether some languages are not more beautiful than others is quite another question. The ugly words are the words not fitted for the company in which they find themselves. There are words which are ugly because of newness or of antiquation; there are words which are ugly because of foreignness or ill-breeding (*e.g.*, Television); but I do not believe that any word well established in our language is either beautiful or ugly."

With these dogmatic statements I am in disagreement. I do find certain words beautiful in themselves; I do not believe that words are ugly for any of the reasons Mr. Eliot offers. The age of words is no bar to their beauty; some of the loveliest words in English are antiquated. Finally, what has its foreignness to do with a word's beauty or ugliness?

When we say that a word is beautiful in itself, we presumably mean that the sound or sight of it gives us pleasure. More often than not, we are thinking of the sound, as in such place-names as I have already mentioned; the name Shenandoah makes music. I will say *this:* sometimes when we examine a word which delights by its combination of certain vowels and consonants, we are likely to find that it has associations for us which are part of its appeal.

Consider, for example, the word *wilderness.* To me it is a beautiful word, but how much is that to be accounted for by the fact that it has a happy conjunction of vowels and consonants, and how much by the fact that I have a great love for wild places, and that it makes me happy to be in them? A while back I mentioned a preference for "*still* waters" over "*quiet* waters." How much, I now ask myself, is that preference due to a quality resident in the word itself, and how much to the long association in my mind of "*still* waters" with one of loveliest of the Psalms?

Dr. Wilfred Funk, who has written interestingly on word origin, once made a list of what he considered the most beautiful words in English. These were his choices: *tranquil, golden, hush, bobolink, thrush, lullaby, chimes, murmuring, luminous, damask, cerulean, melody, marigold, jonquil, oriole, tendril, myrrh, mignonette, gossamer, fawn, dawn, chalice, anemone, alyssum, mist, oleander, amaryllis, rosemary, camellia, asphodel* and *halcyon.* They make an arresting selection, yet some of these words, it seems to me, are dependent primarily or at least equally upon association for their appeal. *Tranquil,* certainly, is not an ugly word, but is it, to choose another word approximate to it in sound, more pleasing to the ear than *thankful?* Does it not gain a great deal from its meaning? We may be thankful and yet disturbed, but tranquillity is a more enviable state. Is *golden* more beautiful than *silvery?* But are we not likely to have a preference as between gold and silver objects, regardless of their comparative value, and might not our choice of one word over the other for inclusion in such a list, be influenced accordingly?

Why should *hush* be given priority over *lush,* save for the fact that the first summons up more agreeable associations? And surely *thrush* has no more beauty in sound than *brush* or *crush;* we see or hear the word, and it brings to mind the bird's song; its beauty lies in association. Or is *chimes* a more lovely word than *climbs?* Here again we are moved by suggestion, and surely the same is true of *damask.* I am not even certain, the more I think about it, as to *dawn,* which has always seemed to me one of the most beautiful of English words. Am I deceiving myself when I argue that the word itself, apart from the memories we have of sunrise, suggests the slow spreading of light? Or that *dusk,* which I like equally well, of itself suggests the slow failing of that light?

A few of Dr. Funk's choices appear to owe their selection simply to the pleasure we derive from their sound. I think this is true of *murmuring, luminous, cerulean, anemone, alyssum, amaryllis, asphodel,* and *chalice.* In the case of *melody,* I would guess that its innate harmony is matched by its pleasing connotation, and that the same is true of *gossamer.* As for *mignonette,* that seems to me merely a pretty word, and I find it hard to understand why Dr. Funk should have included *bobolink.* The condor is a much less attractive bird, but the word by which we name it seems to me more pleasing in sound. The starling is now regarded as among the most pestiferous of birds, yet surely it carries a name no less delightful than *darling.*

Suppose we turn for a moment to the animals, none of which achieved a place on Dr. Funk's list, though they are at least as fortunately named as the birds. *Leopard* comes first to my mind, then *panther,* with *lion* and *tiger* also surely in the van. Indeed, the big cats would appear to have the best of it so far as Adam's naming of the beasts is concerned. And, of course, *rhinoceros* and *hippopotamus,* while not words of beauty, are indisputably appropriate names for the odd creatures they stand for. Who was it said that *cellar door* makes one of the loveliest sounds in English? And by that token, I think we would have to find a place for *polar bear.* I will spare you naming of the fish, except to note that the dolphin seems more happily named than most.

The fact is, that the impact of words upon us, whether we consider them singly or in their proximity to others, is a baffling matter. C. E. Montague once asked, "Why are we moved so strongly and as strangely as we are by certain simple groupings of a few ordinary words?" He observed that some of the finest lines ever written are almost bare of any applied ornament, "anything we can detach and define." How, he asked, are we to analyze the charm of such lines as those of Thomas Nashe;

25

Brightness falls from the air;
Queens have died young and fair;
Dust hath closed Helen's eye.

or Byron's:

She walks in beauty, like the night
Of cloudless climes and starry skies, . . .

It is better not attempted. Few intellectual operations are
capable of being more tiresome than a detailed explanation
or analysis of why something is beautiful. Rarely, a sympa-
thetic critic of the kind recently in disrepute, can flash a
beam of illumination. There is, as Montague went on to say,
"a kind of dazzling unreason" about the effect upon us of
certain conjunctions of words, "a power of taking you captive without giving you any materials for a presumable explanation of your surrender." One of the fascinations of
words is that, like the origin of language itself, they are
shrouded in mystery. All we know is that by some means not
always definable, great writers are able to pass on, so that
we are affected by it, a certain intensity in their own
thought or feeling.

No writer of an age which had none too delicate an ear
was more sensitive to words than the late Walter de la
Mare. Among his other achievements, he produced one of
the finest anthologies in all literature, *Come Hither*. It is distinguished not only for the excellence of its selections from
British and American poetry, but for the extraordinary interest of its notes and comments, which are delightfully dis-
cursive. De la Mare was fascinated by the names for things
—for places, for wildflowers, herbs, for precious stones, and
for the stars. Of these last he wrote, "By strange good fortune
—even apart from such honest homely terms as the Plough,

the Pointers, the Guards, the Chair—the stars have been starrily named. These, for example: Merak, Megrez, Alcor, Alphacca, Alarneb, Dubhe, Markab, Murfrid, Almirzam, Alpheratz, Alphard, Zosma, Denebola, Fomalhaut. They are not only good names for stars, just as Kit Marlowe or Richard Lovelace or Geoffrey Chaucer is a good name for an English poet; or Tycho Brahe or Johannes Hevelius or Giovanni Donati is for an astronomer; or Vasco da Gama, Magellan or Francis Drake is for an adventurer; or Diego Rodríguez de Silva Velásquez is for a painter; but they mean as well as they sound. Nor can you ever be utterly alone, however dark the way, if you can see but one star shining and can call it by name.

"A good name," wrote De la Mare, "is a difficult thing to come by—a name that sounds well, sounds right, and whose meaning continues to fit it however far one chases it through its etymological origins. For apt sound alone only a flash of intuitive insight (especially in a child) can instantly suit word to sight or maybe to hearing (*timbrel, trombone, bassoon*); to touch (*slimy, plush, velvet*); to taste (*syrup, caramel, myrrh, blancmange*); to smell (*bergamot, musk*)." As for the aromatic herbs, their very names, he thought, "seem to perfume the air." He had in mind *bergamot, lavender, meadowsweet, rosemary, woodruff, balm,* and *germander.*

He felt very strongly about the names for flowers. "It would be a pretty courtesy," he suggested, "when the learned converse with the vulgar, if they translated their Latin into intelligible English. When ever a botanist names a flower he mentions only its kind or variety—and that only in reference to some, but by no means to all, of its characteristics. It is important, then, to keep on reminding oneself that every living thing is not merely something which belongs to a family, species, genus, but is unique—itself only, and no other." He then goes on to list some of the country names for English wildflowers—"names always lively, often humorous and sometimes curiously beautiful—but in danger nowadays of dying of disuse. To discover *why* each of these flowers has been so named would be an enthralling but laborious adventure." To choose but one or two examples: Solomon's-seal is known also as David's Harp, Fraxinella, Ladder-to-Heaven and Lily-of-the-Mountain; and Foxglove as Dead-Man's Bell, Fingerflower, Flapdock, and Lusmore.

It may not be amiss to note De la Mare's comment to the effect that "of all names, perhaps those which grammarians have given to the various species of words themselves are the most unalluring: *adjective, adverb, preposition, conjunction,* for example."

De la Mare's disgust with grammatical terms brings to mind how the playwright Edward Sheldon, in company with his oculist, once amused himself by listing the most hideous words in English. They decided that no such list would be complete without *intelligentsia, funeral parlor, housewife,* and *galluses.* Judging from these nominations, I can't believe that Sheldon and his friend gave the matter more than momentary thought, and certainly they were more concerned with the connotations of words than with their sound or their visual appeal. "Funeral parlor" qualifies as a hideous word chiefly because it carries nice Nellieism to a loathsome degree. Still worse, to my mind, is the phrase now so prevalent, "funeral home," an ultimate in verbal absurdity which disfigures the streets of every American town and city.

And what about *housewife?* It is, I grant, by no means a glamorous or exciting word, but it is an honest one, although I suspect it is a term not prized by many women. *Galluses,* to me, wears a humorous and stoutly homespun air. It has a

28

lot more flavor than *suspenders,* which is, however, more descriptive. Our English friends, of course, prefer *braces,* which strikes me as merely an inaccurate word.

What, we might ask before naming some, are the qualities that make certain words ugly? They must vary considerably, I think, both in kind and degree, according to the temperament and tastes, the susceptibilities and sensitivities of the person exposed to them. For my own part, I would place first on the list of these qualities that of disagreeable sound. None of Edward Sheldon's aversions seem to me indictable for that reason. All his hated words come smoothly to the tongue, nor do they grate upon the ear. They are not beautiful, or even pretty; they are innocuous so far as euphony goes, though the hissing sound of *galluses* is no asset. *Intelligentsia,* as a matter of fact, has rather a rippling sound. And equally important with sound, it seems to me, is the power in a word to evoke disgusting or otherwise repellent sensations.

If we permit ourselves to stray outside the boundaries of English, we could come up with some horrendous examples from the German, which, while capable of lovely sounds, can also produce some whose ugliness is hard to match in English: *shrechlichkeit,* for example, or, for that matter, pleasant as its connotations are, *gesundheit.* Even French, that aristocrat of languages, yields some distasteful words. *Crepuscule,* beloved though it has been by many poets, at least when adopted into English as the adjective "crepuscular," is scarcely a thing of beauty.

For a mildly hideous word, how about *polygamous?* Attractive as it may be in its connotations, it is surely not auditorily entrancing. *Pneumococcus* is a likely candidate, as are other words denoting those pestiferous small organisms which make continual warfare upon us. A special niche might be reserved for such words as *mortician* and *beautician,* and another special compartment for such contraptions as *snaggle-toothed.* Even worse than these, I think, is a word that stands for loveliness—*pulchritudinous.* If you looked like Marilyn Monroe and did not know English very well, and somebody called you that, would you think you were being complimented?

In what I have thus far said about ugly words, I have been concerned only with those which are in more or less common use. If one goes further afield, it is, of course, easy to come up with even more frightful examples. In a brief recent gallop through a dictionary I came upon the word *prococuranteism,* hitherto happily unknown to me. Like so many other top-heavy Latinities, I doubt that it has ever sallied forth from the dictionary—and why should it, for what it means is the attitude or behavior characteristic of a person who can be more briefly and more euphoniously described as a trifler. In any case, I think it may fairly be listed as a definitely hideous word.

Several years ago I made the acquaintance, via correspondence, of a retired Baltimore physician, Dr. J. E. Schmidt, who now practices what began as an avocation; he is a professional word consultant, which is not only a unique occupation, but is made the more extraordinary by the fact that Dr. Schmidt derives so much pleasure from this activity that he charges nothing for his services; at least that was true when I last heard from him. Like his late fellow Baltimorean, H. L. Mencken, Dr. Schmidt keeps an enormous file in the pursuit of his hobby. But while Mencken's obsession centered chiefly (aside from his interest in quotations) about the American variants of English, Dr. Schmidt takes all words for his province, and the more esoteric they are the greater seems to be their appeal for him. He delights in such specimens as *emphaloskepsis, proceleusmatic, nepionic, anfractuous* and *steatopygic.*

Dr. Schmidt undertakes to supply his clients with the special words they are looking for. Is there, you might ask him, one word in English designating a redheaded woman of uncertain age, bowlegged, and with a perceptible squint? If the word exists, which God forbid, it will probably be in Dr. Schmidt's file. To illustrate by a more reasonable example: suppose you are hunting for the term standing for the old deathbed habit of picking at the bedclothes; Dr. Schmidt will inform you that the word is *floccillation.*

The Greeks, who are reputed to have had a word for everything, may not have had one for the habit of biting one's fingernails, but there is one in English. So, too, there are words to designate the fear of cats, the sound made by a beetle, or the aspect of the moon when it is less than full but more than half full. You may recall that Shakespeare, whose vocabulary exceeded that of any other writer in English, used the last of these—*gibbous.*

It is obvious that the more words a writer knows, the better, provided he does not try to use them all; but there are, it seems to me, grave dangers inherent in the possibility that others besides writers may begin beating a path to Dr. Schmidt's door. Politicians and statesmen, for example, know far too many words already, and use them much too freely. Observe how nicely those who had their political education in Moscow seem to get along by limiting themselves to a single word, which is, moreover, one of the shortest in their or any other language. Indeed, the present public passion for enlarged vocabularies has its sinister aspects; if indiscriminately satisfied, it can land us into even worse pickles than those in which we are now embrined.

Creative writers may never know too many words, but reviewers and critics would be far more effective, particularly those who bow solemnly to one another in our more erudite quarterlies, if their vocabularies were cut in half. Reviewers are forever being taunted with working certain terms to death. Some years ago it was *adumbrate;* now they cannot write a line without dragging in *perceptive*. Why, we say, can't they find a few new adjectives to replace *civilized* and *adult,* a few more nouns besides *saga* and *canvas* and *texture,* a few more verbs besides *grip* and *explore?* Nonsense! They use too many words as it is, when so often one, and frequently a four-letter word at that, would suffice.

To go back for a moment to such words as we may call beautiful in themselves. Do not suppose that in contending they exist, I am making a plea for the use of a poetic vocabulary in poetry; Wordsworth destroyed that illusion long ago. But I do make my stand with Coleridge, when he defined good prose as the use of proper words in their proper places, and good poetry as the use of the most proper words in their proper places. That is what the translator of the Psalms did when he wrote "beside the still waters."

I V

Clichés and
Curious Expressions

ALL OF US, in conversation or in writing, make use from time
to time of certain long-established phrases with whose exact
meaning or origin we are not always familiar. Those whose
edge has been dulled by constant repetition we call clichés.
For a time, thanks to Gelett Burgess, who coined the word,
we also called them bromides, a term not often used today.
Though clichés are most often best avoided, I do not hold
with those who would place them all in limbo. Some can
occasionally be made to play an unexciting but useful role,
and may even be preferable to an overly self-conscious effort
to avoid them.

Usually it is the cliché which in its origin was most striking in effect that grates most harshly now upon our ears, and offends us even more when we encounter it in print. When certain words were first placed in conjunction, they were a creative act, and because their effect was so striking, they passed at once into common adoption, and rapidly became done to death. Such phrases as "beggars description," "baptism of fire," "fall on deaf ears," "imagination runs riot" and "skate on thin ice," to name but a few, were happy and imaginative combinations of words when they were first put together, but they have gathered mold and lost their vitality, just as a catch phrase in advertising does, so that we recoil from them as much as we do from the repetitive hammering on our ears of certain TV commercials.

Yet there are, I think, some homely bromides, such as "bite off more than one can chew," which still retain something of their pristine freshness and vigor. Then too, there are some long-coupled words which have become so integrated that they amount in effect to a single word; they are not true clichés. Such a phrase is "sooner or later." When I used it not long ago in my column in the New York *Times*, a correspondent questioned my use of it, not on the grounds of its familiarity, but because of the form employed. It was the form in which the phrase ordinarily appears, but my correspondent asked if it would not more properly be written, "soon or late." I had to confess that I had never given any thought to the matter. If you do stop to think about it, "soon or late" would seem to have logic on its side. For if you say, "sooner or later," precisely what do you mean? Sooner than when, later than when? "Soon or late" is precise and clear. Fowler, strangely, is silent about the matter in his classic *Modern English Usage;* so, too, are Bergen and Cornelia Evans in *A Dictionary of Contemporary American Usage.* Mencken preferred "soon or late," and so too have some other discriminating writers. I subscribe myself a convert to the shorter form.

About the same time I was reproved on my use of this phrase, I stumbled into more hot water for the sense in which I had used "independent as a hog on ice." This simile I would include among those homely but unoffending clichés I have already mentioned, but the objections were not based upon the frequency of its use; they were concerned with its meaning. I had intended it as a term of compliment applied to Robert Frost. Not so, cried the objectors; nothing is more helpless than a porker who has been so foolish as to venture out on the frozen surface of a pond. To clinch the argument, one reader sent me a photograph of a most pitiable pig in that predicament. He was, obviously, in a state of terror and collapse.

But to get to the truth of the matter, we shall have to look beyond that convincing photograph, for the origin of the phrase has long been a subject for conjecture and debate. Those who cannot free themselves from such evidence as the photograph presented, logically conclude that the meaning of the phrase must properly be derisive, and that when you speak of someone as being "independent as a hog on ice," you are calling him cocky and overconfident.

The lexicographer, Charles Earle Funk, made an extensive inquiry into the origin of this phrase, and recorded his findings in a book for which it furnished the title—*A Hog On Ice and Other Curious Expressions*. In the 1933 Supplement to the *Oxford English Dictionary*, he found the phrase defined as "denoting awkwardness or insecurity," and the United States given as the country of its origin. Two quotations follow the phrase in the *O.E.D.*, and they are symptomatic of the disagreement that exists regarding its meaning. The first is from a Vermont paper of 1894: "How would

35

a Hackney look going around the track after old Highland Gray? 'Like a hog on ice.' " The second was taken from Carl Sandburg's poem, "The Windy City," in *Slabs of the Sunburnt West* (1922): "Chicago fished from its depths a text: Independent as a hog on ice." He was using the phrase, of course, in praise of his city's self-confidence.

Mr. Funk was unable to find in other reference books anything which threw light on the mystery, and began questioning his friends and acquaintances. Some of the younger ones had never heard the expression, but when he plied older generations with the question, he found that not only did nearly all of them know it, but that the localities in which they had heard the phrase included all the Northern states from Maine to Illinois, and many of those in the South; in Georgia *pig* was more frequently heard than *hog*. Next he sent an inquiry to the Department of Agriculture's Bureau of Animal Industry, asking for information regarding the matter of a hog's maneuverability on the ice. The facts, he was told, are these: "a hog on a smooth icy surface cannot move about in a normal manner. The pads on the feet are smooth and offer no resistance to slippery or smooth icy surfaces. His feet slide out from under him, the legs will either spread as the animal sprawls out on the ice, or they will be drawn under him. In either case, after several attempts to arise, he refuses to try to get on his feet. The hog usually has to be skidded or dragged off the ice to a firm footing before he attempts to move about in the usual manner."

Perhaps it was the phrasing, "hog on ice," rather than "hog on *the* ice," a form in which it has never appeared, that suggested a meat-packing origin to two Midwestern scholars consulted by Mr. Funk. Such an explanation seemed reasonable to me also, until I read Mr. Funk's reminder that refrigeration was not practiced by the meat packers until about 1880, by which date the phrase had been in currency for some time. Further inquiry brought the information that, in spite of the fact that no ice forms in Ireland and that hogs are called pigs there, many older Irish people were familiar with the phrase. It began to look as though the saying had been an importation, both to the United States and to Ireland. English authorities thought it unlikely that England could have been the source, for the same reasons which eliminated Ireland; ice forms rarely in England and a hog is known as a pig.

Where then, did the phrase come from? Mr. Funk got the lead he was looking for when he learned that "a hog on ice" was known and used by old-timers in northern England, and particularly by their Scottish acquaintances. He made an imaginative leap. He was aware from his dictionary studies that in the ancient Scottish game of curling, the word *hog* is used to describe a curling stone which has not been given sufficient impetus by a player, and comes to rest before reaching its intended mark. As to why it was so called, the *Century Dictionary* noted, "Origin obscure; by some identified with hog (*i.e.,* swine), 'laggard stones that manifest a pig-like indolence,' or, it might be though, in allusions to the helplessness of a hog on ice, there being in the United States an ironical simile, 'as independent as a hog on ice'!" This, in 1889, was the earliest reference to the phrase that Mr. Funk was able to find in print.

No investigator is more determined, more unremitting in his efforts to track down the object of his search than a lexicographer in quest of the origin of a word or phrase. He will spend amazing effort to satisfy himself, and so with Mr. Funk. For a while he thought that this curling stone "afforded an ideal explanation of the phrase, that the 'hog,' lying indolently upon the course, was free and independent, by its immobile state blocking the way of subsequent stones to be played, forming a hazard." Then, reading the rules of the game, he discovered that the "hog" is required to be removed from the course as soon as it comes to rest.

Frustrated once more, he turned to the history of the game, which dates back at least to the early sixteenth century. As with all games, he considered, the rules change from time to time over the years. And so he came to a conclusion; he could not prove its truth, but it seemed credible to him that sometime during the game's early history—and by accident, perhaps—one of the rather awkward stones first used lacked momentum to reach its destination and stopped short of it. Then someone proposed that it be allowed to stay there as an extra hazard, and that because of its unwieldiness and inertia, some player likened it to a hog.

"If this hypothesis be correct," he writes, "then the very fact that the stone occupied a central position, showing no regard to its interference with subsequent players, like an automobile driver who 'hogs' the center of a road, made it appear self-assured, cocky, and independent, and this gave rise to the humorous simile that came down through the centuries." It is an ingenious explanation, and one I am ready to accept.

Not all searches for the origin of a familiar phrase are as interesting as Mr. Funk's quest of the "hog," but there are some expressions in current use which might provide a happy time for the dedicated investigator. For example, a few years ago, in a column about dictionaries, I suggested that the ordinary dictionary would be an even more interesting book than it is if it contained a supplement devoted to phrases in common current use, with their equivalents in earlier periods. I mentioned that I had been trying to establish, in my memory at least, when that popular and to many ears annoying phrase, "good-by now," came into common use. My guess was that it did not much antedate World War II; at least I could not remember having heard it earlier. Also I speculated as to *why* it came into being, suspecting that it was the natural outgrowth of the constant effort in English to find a satisfactory substitute for the finality which *good-by*, over the centuries, has assumed. As a contraction of "God be with you" I doubt that in the beginning it had the same quality of finality. English has no established phrase comparable to the French *au revoir*, the Italian *a rivederci*, the German *auf wiedersehen*. Consequently we have invented slang or colloquial phrases which do not live beyond the comparatively brief periods in which they are commonly used. A short while ago it was "so long," which is now not so often heard; today it is either "good-by now," or "I'll be seeing you," or, among men particularly, "Take it easy." The first, it seems to me, attempts to ease the finality of *good-by*, by assuming a more temporary air; the second has the sense of the foreign phrases just quoted; and the last might be accounted for as the natural product of a hurried, stressful period. Curiously, forms of greeting seem to change less often than the phrases used for parting. Aside from the formal "how do you do?" or the more casual "how are you?", "hello" still holds its own, though the monosyllabic "hi!" has taken over pretty completely among youngsters and is frequently used by their elders as well.

These speculations brought some interesting correspondence, and even though I have not pursued them with the diligence of Mr. Funk, the letters I received did seem to establish that both "good-by now" and "take it easy" have had a longer life than I first imagined. "Good-by now" apparently antedates World War II by ten or fifteen years, and seems to have reached New York from other localities where it was often used. There is ground for belief that it is Irish-American in origin; apparently it gained wider and more frequent currency in South Boston, and in certain Pennsylvania towns with a large Irish population, than elsewhere. As evidence of its use in Ireland before its adoption here, I was referred to a brief passage in Joyce's *Ulysses,* in which Buck Mulligan says, "Good-by, now, good-by. Write down all I said and tell Tom, Dick and Harry. . . . Good-by, now, good-by."

Horace Reynolds, a word aficionado of long and high standing, made the amusing suggestion that the phrase was born out of the Irishman's inclination to prolong conversation, his "disinclination to stop talking and take his farewell." He mentioned that Mencken, in his *American Language,* suggests that we may well have acquired our fondness for intensive prefixes and suffixes from the Irish, instancing as examples *no-siree* and *yes-indeedy.* The Irishman, Mr. Reynolds pointed out, "finds it hard to say a simple no or yes, as well as a simple good-by. This, I think, is as much a part of the instinct for politeness as for palaver. 'Yes,' like 'good-by,' seems too naked and bald. So he adds a sootherin' extra word, and comes up with 'good-by now' and 'yes-indeedy.' "

Another correspondent called attention to the fact that "good-by now" is predominantly used by women, and attributed their widespread use of it to their hatred of finality. Though it is used more frequently, in my observation, by women, just as "take it easy" is more often a masculine phrase, I have heard enough men say "good-by now" to render shaky the foundation for my correspondent's explanation. I think the constant use of these words is simply one more reflection of the need for an equivalent to the European phrases.

As for "take it easy," is it not reasonable to suppose that it took its rise among men working together at manual labor? It probably had its origin in the days when hours were longer than now, and one laborer, aware that the secret of completing the day's work without being done in was to maintain a steady but easygoing pace, would shout these words of caution to another. There is the old English saying, "easy does it," though that phrase has never been used as a formula for parting. So far, I have been unable to determine just when "take it easy" entered into common usage.

"Dead as a doornail" is one of those familiar phrases which are constantly used without any idea of how they came to have the meaning we attach to them. Why a doornail should be considered so moribund was a puzzle to me until a correspondent, Mr. Rex Lampman, shed some light on its probable origin. He pointed out that doornails have always been driven over their heads into the doorjamb, and the holes left by the sunken heads then filled with putty to be painted over, thus leaving no trace of the doornail. He suggested that carpenters are more to be relied upon in this matter than etymologists. The phrase is very old. I remember first coming upon it in Dickens, but in Shakespeare's *Henry IV*, Part 2, Act V, Scene 3, Falstaff exclaims, "What! is the old king dead!" and Pistol replies, "As nail in door." And more than two centuries earlier (about 1350), we find in *The Parlement of the Three Ages*, so Mr. David Guthrie informs me, an alliterative poem in which a poet-poacher describes the hunting of a hart in the woods at dawn, ending with these two lines:

And happened that I hitt hym be-hynde the left sholdire.
Dead as a dornayle was he fallen.

Now I wait for some industrious scholar to come up with the information that the same expression can be found in the ancient Anglo-Saxon or Celtic bards.

Another teasing familiar phrase is "keep a stiff upper lip." The Evanses rightly observe that it is the lower lip which trembles when we are overly perturbed, and I suspect that the explanation of the phrase which was offered me by Mr. James Crawford is more ingenious than dependable. If, he suggested, it is American in origin, and dates back about a hundred years, as some authorities maintain, might it not have been touched off by the Civil War powder cartridge, which was opened with the front upper teeth? He pointed out that many men are said to have tried to escape arms-bearing service by knocking out these teeth.

In *A Hog On Ice and Other Curious Expressions,* and in *Heavens to Betsy! And Other Curious Sayings* Mr. Funk has traced the history of many familiar phrases. So too has Webb B. Garrison in *Why You Say It.* Mr. Garrison delved, for example, into the history of "putting on the dog." It is an expression that was more common in my childhood than it is today, but it has been a familiar part of American speech for several generations. We are more likely now to say *ritzy* and let it go at that. Mr. Garrison found that "putting on the dog" came into use during the period of great material expansion following the Civil War, when fortunes were being rapidly made, and the display of new wealth took many new forms. Lap dogs became very popular among the wives of the new millionaires, and gradually "putting on the dog" became synonymous with lavish display. By 1885 it was in common use.

I had always supposed that the phrase "to go west" had its origin in World War I, when it was so frequently used, especially among the British, as a synonym for dying. Actually its origin is centuries old. In the thirteenth century a great new prison was built near Newgate, the western gate made by the Romans in London's city wall, and when Newgate prisoners were condemned to death, they were led out the gate and due west to Tyburn. By 1592 the phrase was in general use in the sense given such wide currency during World War I.

Older still in origin is the metaphorical phrase we use when we speak of "washing our hands" of a matter. The ancient Biblical plays frequently had for one of their scenes the enactment of Jesus' trial before Pilate. It was customary to bring in a basin, and have Pilate wash his hands before the audience as he denied responsibility for the death sentence. And "a far cry" goes back to medieval Scottish times. Couriers bearing local messages were said to be given "a near cry," but when, in times of national emergency, a crier might have to ride long distances, the phrase "a far cry" came into being.

To return to the cliché proper—a category to which I think it unfair to assign certain homely phrases which have never worn out their welcome—Fowler, who in his *Modern English Usage* preferred to use the term "hackneyed phrase," estimated the number of indubitable clichés in the hundreds. Bergen and Cornelia Evans number them in thousands. Certainly clichés constantly multiply, and perhaps they find the American soil especially friendly to growth. At any rate, the Evanses give them more attention than they have received in any comparable reference book, and they discuss at least two hundred of them.

Now we all know that the cliché, too frequently relied on, can ruin writing and disfigure speech, yet I believe that both Fowler and the Evanses are overly severe in their treatment of the habit. They are severe, of course, in a good

43

cause. There must be constant war on the cliché. If the language is not to be overwhelmed by dry rot, it must always renew itself, and it is in the making from day to day. Yet some of these tired phrases serve humble but honorable purposes. And offensive as they sometimes are, it is possible for the reader to be equally annoyed by a too strained effort to achieve freshness. Writers need to guard against both pressures.

In their concern with the cliché, the Evanses have turned up some very interesting material. Besides calling attention to the part which alliteration has played in gaining currency for such hoary survivals as "beat about the bush," "fit as a fiddle," and "death's door," they point out that many of these phrases have won wide circulation even when their exact meaning is puzzling.

As perhaps the outstanding example of a familiar phrase for which we are completely unable to account, they cite "drug on the market." We know, of course, the meaning that has become attached to it, but what were the circumstances which gave it that meaning? It may be, as the Evanses suggest, that the term had its origin in some long-forgotten pun. It has been in constant use since 1661, when it is believed to have first appeared, but in all the years since we have become none the wiser regarding the reasons for its inception.

Another peculiarity of clichés is that the range of our individual reactions to them is very wide. Not everyone is equally disturbed by this or that familiar grouping of words. All of us can cite certain phrases we would be happy never to see or hear again, but we have differing levels of tolerance. There are some clichés, of course, on which an almost unanimous vote for banishment could be taken. Among these I would place "add insult to injury," "rest upon one's laurels," "an infinite capacity for taking pains," and "conspicuous by his absence." Such a list would include some of the most apt and clever phrases ever penned, like "the long arm of coincidence." We may shudder when we encounter it, but how good it was in the beginning!

As I have already suggested, there are certain workaday phrases, classed as clichés, which it would be difficult to do without, and which because of their great compression have in effect become words rather than phrases. Toward these I think we can afford a greater tolerance than some guardians of the language seem willing to grant. In some measure the Evanses, for example, concede this point, but grudgingly. They argue that usually there are single words which would serve same purpose; I would reply that often they are not as effective. Can we spare "put back the clock," or "at loose ends," or "mark time," or "change of heart"? Take even such a phrase as "benefit of the doubt." The Evanses counsel against its use, both in speech and writing, but it seems to me that so much has been compressed in it that to use it is preferable to the involved exposition that would otherwise be called for.

With the exceptions I have noted, and which seem to me valid, there has been no better summing up of the arguments for and against clichés than that offered by Eric Partridge in *A Charm of Words*: "In the interplay of conversation, a cliché is often redeemed by a moue or a shrug or an accomplice-smile: 'There, I've used a cliché. Very careless and humdrum of me, I suppose. But at least you know what I mean.' Intonation, pauses, emphasis, these and other means can invest a cliché-ridden sentence, or set of sentences, with humour and wit, and with realism and trenchancy. In writing, we lack these dramatic, these theatrical, these extraneous aids: we *stand or fall alone*. In writing, the battered simile and the forgotten metaphor may well be ludicrous or

45

inept or repellent; the hackneyed phrase so commonplace
that it offends, the idiom so weak that it enfeebles the argument or dulls the description or obscures the statement; the
foreign phrase either so inadequate or so out of place that it
sets up a misgiving, a doubt, a dissent; the quotation so
mauled by the maudlin, so coy in the mouths of the prim,
so bombastic in the speech of the pompous, as to be risible,
so very common as to lose all distinction, so inept as to fail.
'If in doubt, don't.' "

The more one contemplates the cliché, the more one becomes aware of what an exasperating medium language can
be. It is quicksilver. It is alchemy, constantly changing baser
metals to better, and vice versa. The painter knows where he
is with his colors, and so does the sculptor with his wood or
metal or stone, or the architect with his various materials.
These do not change. But the writer deals with living stuff,
and words, or the combinations we make of them, assume
lives of their own, and alter and die, even before our eyes.

Certain sights and sounds, however often repeated, remain always arresting. The crescent moon, cascading water,
the evening star, the first flush of day in the east, the sound
of bells over summer fields, train whistles in the loneliness of
the night (once upon a time)—of these we never tire. But
words, our greatest creation, are corrupted by time and use.
They are tricky characters; they start out by meaning one
thing, and end up, as often as not, by meaning something
quite different. They may begin shabbily and acquire
glamor, or take off by parading themselves in drawing
rooms, only to end up in the gutter. Take such a verb as *can-
vass*, which had its birth, according to the *O.E.D.*, in 1508.
The variety of its history is amazing. When it came into the
language, it had a meaning approximate to the sense in
which we now use it: to solicit, as support, votes, orders,

46

contributions, etc. But not many years later it could mean to toss in a canvas sheet, to knock about, to beat or to batter. About the same time it was used figuratively as meaning to buffet in writing, to criticize destructively, and, later still, to bargain with. In the eighteenth century it came to mean to sue for something. Now we use it as it was used in the early years of the last century—in a return to its original meaning—and all the other meanings it acquired over the centuries have dropped away. Its sense has become restricted to soliciting the support of a constituency, or ascertaining the number of one's supporters.

How, one wonders, do lexicographers keep their sanity?

V

A Shrewdness of Apes

Several years ago, referring in an article to a passing bout of illness, I made use of the phrase, "a bevy of inconsiderate bacteria." I used the word *bevy* because I could think of no commonly accepted group designation for microorganisms; there is, to be sure, the laboratory term, *culture*, but that is properly applied to prepared bacteria, whereas the maleficent particles which had laid me low were enjoying a completely independent life when I encountered them.

Afterward, the act of having chosen that particular word set me to thinking about various group designations used in English, particularly those applied to living things. It amused me to note how incongruous, and even how grotesque, these terms can become when they are misapplied. We speak, for example, of a *herd* of elephants, and employ the same word with reference to large groups of other big animals, like the buffalo. We do not use it in referring to lions or tigers simply because the great cats, like their smaller cousins, do not move about in large companies. If we transfer the term to dogs, let us say, which in the wild state, at least, may be found together in such numbers that we speak of a *pack,* the effect of *herd* would be merely incongruous. But if we were to speak of a herd of mice (which no one has ever seen), the effect would be not only incongruous, but ludicrous as well.

There is a kind of logic about some group designations. One imagines, for example, that the noun *flock,* as applied to birds, came later than the same word used as a verb, it having been observed that birds tend to flock together. The word *school* as applied to fish made no sense to me until I discovered that it was derived from various words meaning multitude or troop. As in the case of so many other words, group terms have, in some instances, shifted in their application through the course of time. I was surprised to find that *pack* was sometimes used in the seventeenth century as a group term for birds, particularly grouse. *Flock* was at one time applied to animals of various kinds, feeding or traveling in company; now, aside from birds, we confine it to sheep, and occasionally goats. Likewise, *school,* which we now reserve for fish—and sometimes whales—was in the sixteenth century applied to various animals. And *bevy,* which started this whole train of thought, has itself enjoyed a wide application, which may excuse my use of it in connection with bacteria. Properly, it is reserved for pleasant assemblages— quail, larks and roes, and, of course, maidens.

The word *swarm,* I was pleased to discover, has been rigidly confined to insects and human beings. Deriving obviously from the habits of both species, it was first applied to bees, but has been extended to embrace locusts, mosquitoes, ants, and *Homo sapiens;* plainly, it has become a group designation for pests, though that is doing a gross injustice to the bee. I am aware that ants, who invented the oversized city, foolishly adopted by man, are spoken of as comprising *colonies,* but *swarm,* when we think of ants, is the word that comes first to mind. I had almost forgotten another exclusive word of this kind, which is *covey.* It is the inalienable right of partridges to be so grouped, though the privilege is sometimes extended to grouse and a few other game birds. But even *covey,* I find on consulting the *O.E.D.,* was in the sixteenth century sometimes figuratively used for a family or a party. There is one gathering for which only one word has sanctioned use. Angels in any quantity may be referred to only as a *host.* The word's title to that distinction is clear enough; *host* derives from the Latin *hostis,* meaning enemy, and hence came to mean an army. It was presumably applied to angels as the warriors of God.

Before leaving the human, or superhuman, application of group terms for a closer examination of those used in connection with the lower animal orders, I should like to say a word or two about a phrase that I first encountered in Margaret Mitchell's *Gone With the Wind.* You may recall that when Rhett Butler proposed to Scarlett that she become his mistress, she (ever the realist) exclaimed, "Mistress! What would I get out of that except a passel of brats?" I turned to Harold Wentworth's *American Dialect Dictionary* for some light on the origin of *passel.* I did not find it there in precisely that form, though it does appear as "a hull passel of children," and "a hull passel of young-ones." Mr. Wentworth assigns "a passel of thieves" to the Middle West, "a passel o' folks" and "a passel o' hogs" to the South. Apparently the word has been used to designate a lot of almost anything.

Shortly after I made use of the word *bevy* as applied to bacteria, I was reproved by a correspondent on the indisputable grounds that *bevy* minimizes the incredible numbers in which microorganisms foregather. It was pointed out to me that larks, roebucks, and even maidens, all of which in groups become a bevy, would not be pleasant in astronomical numbers. Somehow these group terms, like many debatable questions regarding words and their usage, arouse violent feelings in their partisans. I have been less than gently reproved for speaking of whales as congregating in herds, and admonished that even as a merely occasional resident of Martha's Vineyard, I should be aware that in New England whaling idiom a cetacean gathering may be acceptably referred to only as a *gam*. This word, which in the great days of whaling was used also for an encounter between two whale ships, appears somewhat disappointingly in Dr. Wentworth's dialect dictionary merely in the sense of a social visit or chat. Of recent years we know it, of course, in its plural form, as a designation for what a pair of nylons enfolds. As a parting word for whales in quantity, it may be added that *pod* has been used to designate conventions of them as well as for walruses, seals, and porpoises.

Among the most widely known and used group terms in the animal kingdom is a *pride* of lions, which seems also one of the most appropriate; the *O.E.D.*'s only comment on this use of the word is, "a fanciful term for a 'company' of lions." Leopards must be content with *lepe*. I have found no group word for tigers, but *clowder* has been used for both wildcats and the domestic variety. Bears in quantity, though they are not gregarious, are slightly referred to as a *sloth*, hogs as a *drift*, wolves not only as a *pack*, but also as a *route.* We have a *stud* of mares, a *haras* of horses, a *rag* of colts, a *husk* of jack rabbits, a *down* of hares, and a *nest* of cottontails. One of the most interesting group terms for animals is that for a congregation of apes—a *shrewdness.* The *O.E.D.* gives *mischievous* as one of the many meanings of *shrewd* (it is an incredibly variegated list). Since mischief is a propensity commonly attributed to simians, one imagines that a *shrewdness* of apes may be so accounted for.

A *barren* of mules, in view of that creature's sterility, is readily understandable; so, too, because in motion they make one think of bulldozers, is a *crash* as applied to rhinoceroses; that plural, by the way, one somehow feels should always be rhinoceri. One of the more amusing, and also apt designations is a *cowardice* of curs.

When we turn to birds, most of us are familiar with a *gaggle* of geese, as we are with a *covey* of quail. Not so well known are a *sedge* of herons, a *spring* of teal, a *walk* of snipe, a *fall* of woodcock, or a *eule* of turtledoves. It puzzles me that I have been unable to find a group term for gulls, which may frequently be seen in great congregations. A few of the collective nouns for birds are both striking and beautiful. I have in mind particularly a *murmuration* of starlings, although Mr. Hal Borland has referred to this one as "a magnificent understatement," a *watch* of nightingales, and finest of all, perhaps, an *ascension* or an *exaltation* of larks.

Many of the terms I have mentioned appeared in medieval "courtesy books," which contained lists of terms that were considered proper for one considering himself to be, or wishing to have himself considered by others to be, a gentleman. These lists were often entitled "Terms of Venery," and the words there included were in more general use then than they are today.

VI

Sound and Substance

IT IS an accepted axiom that poetry is best read aloud.
Though part of the pleasure in reading, content and sub-
stance aside, is obtainable by the eye alone, no good poem
and, I would add, no prose of true excellence, can be fully
savored unless it is heard as well as seen. One may state as a
complementary truth that nothing shows up a shoddy piece
of writing more effectively than reading it aloud. Charles
Townsend Copeland's recognition of that truth was one of
the reasons for his success as a teacher of what was formerly
—and sensibly—known as composition. Copey, as he was
known to generations of Harvard students, made it his in-
variable practice to have his pupils read their work aloud to

him. By that means they learned, if they learned nothing else, that a phrase which comes stumblingly to the tongue is likely also to present greater difficulty to the eye and to the understanding than one in which the flow of sound is smooth and pleasing to the ear.

One reason why the King James version of the Bible has endured through the centuries and can never be displaced —though it may profitably be supplemented and its meaning clarified by modern versions—is that the seventeenth-century translators were men with sensitive ears; they have been unexcelled in the skill with which they juggled vowels and consonants. It is this feeling for the sound of words, whether singly or in combination, which, aside from their content, makes much of the beauty of the Psalms as we read them in the Authorized Version, and makes undying prose of Ecclesiastes, Job, and the Book of Ruth.

Take such a passage as this from the prophet's lament in Jeremiah 6: ". . . the day goeth away, for the shadows of evening are stretched out. . . . I set watchmen over you, saying, Hearken to the sound of the trumpet. But they said, We will not hearken. Therefore hear, ye nations, and know. . . . Hear, O earth: behold I will bring evil upon this people, even the fruit of their thoughts, because they have not hearkened unto my words. . . . To what purpose cometh there to me incense from Sheba, and the sweet cane from a far country? Your burnt offerings are not acceptable, nor your sacrifices sweet unto me."

Note in that passage the unobtrusive use of alliteration, the variety in sentence structure, the ease with which each phrase falls from the lips. Note the splendid instrumentation in the apposition of the vowels and consonants, and then turn to the almost unpronounceable phrases you will encounter in nearly any contemporary textbook on sociology,

54

nearly any government directive (these being among the chief offenders against the potential clarity and beauty of language). Or choose, if you like, a passage from four out of five contemporary novelists; or, more sadly still, poets, and see how seldom this feeling for the texture of words, for the sound they make, is present, whatever other merits the writing may have.

It is true, of course, that the matter of the quality resident in certain vowels and consonants can be pressed to a degree where it becomes preciousness; though one cannot deny that the letter "l" has a liquid quality, that there is force behind the letters "b" and "f" at the beginning of a word, and so on, that their combination with certain vowels produces a certain effect, yet it is possible to carry these delicate shadings too far. Dame Edith Sitwell, who has an exceptionally sensitive ear, does this very often as, in the critical notes interspersed through her anthology of British and American poetry, she analyzes how some poets obtain their effects.

In this connection, it is interesting to observe how often the letters with which a word begins give it a certain character. Ivor Brown has pointed out in one of his fascinating "word anthologies" how frequently, for instance, words beginning with the letters "sm" are of an unpleasant kind. One can easily compile an impressive list of them: we have *smear* and *smut, smirch* and *smudge* and *smug, smell* and *smirk, smoother* and *smash.* It is also worth noting that *smear,* so much in common use today, is not the only one of these words that started out in life under more honorable auspices. *Smear,* originally, had a benign significance, and long ago it denoted the ceremonial act of anointing with oil. *Smirk* once had the meaning of neat or trim, and was so used in Shakespeare's time. *Smug,* too, began its career innocently enough; at first, though it had the same meaning as *smirk* when applied to persons, it also meant smooth and clean when applied to things. Perhaps because so many "sm" words conveyed the idea of dirt, *smatter*, which started out in their company, came to have its present meaning. Since words suffer as much as people from bad company, this generalization about the history of the "sm" words seems a reasonable one.

Elsewhere Mr. Brown has commented on the quite different character that has associated itself with words beginning with "st." Under that grouping we can muster such blood brothers as *sturdy* and *stout, stalwart* and *strong, stiff* and *steady, stubborn* and *stable* (as an adjective). I grant there is one slightly embarrassing impediment to acceptance of this characterization in the presence of the word *stink*, and yet cannot that too be marshaled as corroborative evidence, in view of the fact that the basic quality shared by these words is not beauty but strength?

Confining ourselves for the moment to words beginning with the letter "s," we see that there are still other opening combinations that have an impressive clannishness. Surely it is not accident that we have *slip* and *slide, slink* and *slouch, sluff* and *slither*, all of which share a certain community of motion. And a most imposing list can be compiled out of the words beginning with "sn," all of them notable for a distinctly derogatory tone. Here are *sneak* and *snide, sneer, snooty* and *snotty*, and, for good measure, *sniff* and *snoop, snub* and *snicker*. Even *snore* and *snooze* bear about them a tinge of disapprobation.

Again, is it mere coincidence that we have *scold* and *scoff, scotch* and *scuff, scat* and *scare* and *scrimp* and *scrounge?* Or *scavenge, scathe,* and *scar?* Each is offensive in a double-barreled sense. Surely it is not just a matter of such words

56

merely reproducing their kind. In certain instances, at least, I think it reasonable to assume that these words of a feather came into being because the letter combinations with which they begin are suggestive of the meanings they bear. *Slip* and *slide,* for example, are just as evocative of the action they indicate as *thunder* is of the sound it designates. In the case of the "st" words the suggestiveness is more intangible, but it is present nevertheless. Somehow the combination connotes uprightness and toughness.

I wonder, too, if the manner in which certain letters issue from our lips did not play a part in determining the character of the words formed with them. Think, for a moment, of how forcibly the letter "b" is expelled; it leaves the mouth like a watermelon seed. Then observe how many words beginning with that letter denote the application of force, how many of them match in violence the labial act of forming their initial letter. Thus we have (including some slang words, which are almost habitually expressive) words like *batter* and *blast, bang* and *bust, bruise* and *bump, bend* and *break, butt* and *blow, bounce* and *biff, beat* and *buck.* Shall I mention *bomb?* And somewhat allied with these, surely, are *bold, brazen, brash,* and *blunt.*

Then consider for a moment what happens when the letter in question is formed in the manner of "l." It assumes shape almost imperceptibly, far removed from the explosiveness of "b." And what are its progeny? Words like *lazy* and *loose, limp* and *lost, laggard* and *late,* and *lone.*

Such considerations as these moved Alastair Reid, in an amusing little book called *Ounce, Dice, Trice,* to make lists of light words ("to be said in windy or singing moods") such as *ariel, willow, spinnaker, whirr, lissom, sibilant, petticoat, nimble,* and *nib;* of heavy words ("to be used in gloom or bad weather") like *duffel, blunderbuss, galoshes, bowl, befuddled, mugwump, pumpkin, crumb,* and *blob.* He makes a collection of "squishy words": *squiff, squidge, squamous, squinny, squelch, squash, squeegee, squirt,* and *squab.* Also, he rolls a few of his own collective nouns: "a humbuggle of packages; a giggle of girls; a scribbitch of papers; a snigglement of string; a tribulation of children." He concocts a few words to represent sounds: "Mrraaowl is what cats really say; kinclunk is a car going over a manhole cover; paloop is the tap dripping in the bath." Mr. Reid has names for things, including twins (Helter and Skelter or Pell and Mell for kittens), and, as the title of his book suggests, you can make up your own numbers if you tire of one, two, three.

In the concluding chapter of *A Writer's Notes on His Trade,* C. E. Montague came to what seemed to him the ultimate literary question. All lines of thought about writing, he observed, lead up to the query, "Why are we moved as strongly and as strangely as we are by certain simple groupings of a few ordinary words?" My own conviction is that the answer lies more often in sound than in sense. The so-called New Criticism has done much explication of texts, some of it useful and interesting, some of it useless and boring. For all its patient probing, I think it has seldom given satisfactory answers to Montague's question. It has failed to do so because its approach has been prevailingly intellectual, obsessed as much of the New Criticism has been by the ridiculous notion that such a thing as a science of criticism is possible. This, like the comparable idea of a science of society, is one of the major fallacies of our time. No science can be erected on a foundation of intangibles and variables, prone to the fluctuations of human temperament and the subjective process. Words pass through that process, and as Oliver Cromwell observed when he was asked by Parliament to take the title of king, they "have not their import from the natural power of particular combinations of character, or from the real efficacy of certain sounds, but from the consent of those that use them, and arbitrarily annex certain ideas to them, which might have been signified with equal propriety by any other." Note that Cromwell recognized "the real efficacy of certain sounds."

Our response to those groupings "of a few ordinary words" by which we are so "strongly and strangely" moved, is prevailingly emotional. Sometimes our reaction is touched off by certain arrangements of vowels and consonants (not always as consciously contrived by the writer as they appear to be); or, in verse particularly, the rhythm may be so insistent or so insinuating that the words employed may be difficult to forget. This is one of the reasons why so much of contemporary poetry resists quotation, and is so difficult to remember. In traditional poetry, rhythm was often overstated, and in too obvious a manner; today the fault lies in understatement, much as it does in contemporary acting. These extremes, as Montague remarked, are not to be sneezed at; they are effective. You will find them used in many of Shakespeare's best lines, and they are, indeed, recurrent in the work of nearly every major poet. Yet what of those lines in poetry which seem bare of any device and are nevertheless unforgettable? One thinks of Shakespeare's line:

Childe Roland to the dark tower came—

which, as Montague observes, was left without context "to haunt the minds of poets like one of the isolated granules of beauty surviving from the Greek anthology." For it, too, has the essential gemlike quality—a kind of dazzling unreason, as it may seem at first sight—a power of taking you captive without giving you any materials for a presumable explanation of your surrender. Of this description also is such a poem as Walter de la Mare's "The Traveler," or Robert Frost's "Stopping by Woods on a Snowy Evening." Why, in Frost's poem, is the magic worked by the repetition of the last line, "And miles to go before I sleep"?

All we know is that by some means, not always definable, great writers are able to pass on, so that we are affected by it, a certain intensity in their own thought and feeling. We naturally think of the communication of sounds by radio as mysterious, though it is factually explainable; not so easily can we gauge the means by which words exert their power.

V I I

Notes on Slang

IN THIS ERA of new-won liberties for the written and spoken word, the bars have been let down not only for the employment of four-letter words which had long been social outcasts, but for an ever-widening use of their more respectable cousins, slang phrases. So far as I am aware, no lexicographer has yet written a comprehensive, comparative history of slang. Such a book would demand a wide range of knowledge—mastery of many languages, familiarity with social customs in many countries and periods, and a keen etymological sense—but it could be one of the most interesting books ever written in the field of language. I suspect, without sufficient scholarship to buttress the assumption, that Ameri-

cans have been the most prolific and the most apt practition-
ers in that branch of verbal creation, just as the Germans
have been outstanding in their contribution of scientific and
philosophical terms. German humor may be crude and
heavy-footed, as opposed to the lightness and dexterity of
French wit, the delightful understatement of British humor,
or the rollicking overstatement of its American counterpart
—but each to its own!

I, for one, would like to know what Greek and Egyptian
slang were like, and what the authors of the Old Testament
regarded as slang, and therefore unfit to be used in their
matchless record of a primitive people. As matters stand, we
have only a scanty knowledge of the slang of Shakespeare's
day, and little more of that of the eighteenth century in
English. On the history of our own slang, much has been written, and the accounts, of course, are in need of constant revision, for few things change faster than fashions in slang.
Its persistent use makes for one of the greatest hazards with
which any writer has to contend. George Ade might be better appreciated today if he had not written his fables in
slang, and O. Henry would be still more widely read than he
is if he had not indulged so freely in the argot of his time
and place.

The creation of slang resembles the prodigality of nature,
which is continuous and uninterrupted. Of all the multi-
tudinous seeds that nature sows, only a small fraction arrive at their potential growth. So it is with slang. For a hundred new-minted phrases that catch the public fancy, one
survives, finally to reach conditional permanence in the
pages of a dictionary whose scope is wider than that of slang
itself. Americans of middle age and older remember *Skidoo*
and *Twenty-three, sheeny* and *coon* and *the cat's pajamas,*
but who else does except the compilers of slang dictionaries?

One of the most interesting observations made by Stuart Flexner in his preface to the *Dictionary of American Slang,* on which he collaborated with Harold Wentworth, was that most American slang is created by males. Also, as their book makes abundantly clear, slang, and especially our current slang, is primarily produced by certain subgroups of the population. As Mr. Flexner points out, one reason why slang is predominantly—I would say almost exclusively—of male origin, is that men belong to more of these subgroups than do women.

There are exceptions—in particular, the teen-agers. The boys among them may be the originators, but certainly the composition of the group is almost evenly divided between the two sexes. This is true of certain other subgroups: college students, people in show business, and immigrants. But men do predominate in other subgroups (a term I must use in spite of my hatred of sociological lingo) which Mr. Flexner lists as among the chief current contributors to American slang: the Army, the Navy and Merchant Marine, the underworld, narcotic addicts, jazz musicians and fans, financial-district employees, baseball players and their fans, railroad workers, and hobos.

Many of our slang words are not traceable to such sources, but there is no doubt that today, at least, the greater part of them are the product of special groups. I do not believe that could be said of American slang a century ago when some of these groups did not exist, or, when they did, were less numerous and had less impact on the speech of other people.

In spite of women's entrance into the business and professional worlds, their contacts and, in the majority of instances, the range of their interests are more limited than men's. Their personal relations, as Mr. Flexner observes, still tend to be restricted to family and neighborhood friends, but I think he fails to take into consideration the current range of women's reading, which today is more often wider than that of men. Mr. Flexner also notes that men tend to avoid words that are feminine or weak—poor ingredients for a slang phrase that will stick—and also that men purposely use slang to shock.

There is still another reason for the leading part men play in the creation of slang. Mr. Flexner is no doubt aware of it, although he makes no mention of it in his preface. That reason is that men express their creative drive more diversely than do women. There is no need, surely, to labor men's creative dominance in the worlds of art and science. Slang, to be sure, is a very minor manifestation of this innate capacity, but its origination is definitely a part of it. Men are instinctively innovators, women conservators, and I say this with no intention of derogating women's intelligence. All the fantastic daydreams that man has tried to put into effect have been the creations of the less realistic sex.

There are some other aspects of this matter that interest me very much. Women use the slang which men create, but they, too, bend language in their own way, and the reason they do so is of as much interest as the reason men are the originators of slang. There are many words and phrases used almost exclusively by women which are noticeably absent from the speech of men. These are not slang, but words misapplied. It is true that most of the slang men create rests on hyperbole, which dictionaries define as exaggeration for the sake of effect. But the ordinary speech of women, and of American women in particular, is loaded with overemphasis. More than men, women talk in superlatives, and perhaps with less discrimination. They apply, far beyond the bounds of rationality, such words as *adorable, divine,* and *precious* to objects or ideas which do not warrant their use. They use phrases like "too dreamy for words," "most marvelous," and "couldn't be nicer." The list could be considerably extended.

Why do they do this? I can't offer an answer with complete assurance, but I know some women would say they do so out of a feeling of insecurity, out of an often unvoiced conviction that American men do not take them seriously—that to the American man they are either playthings or impossibly idealized creatures who bear no resemblance to the realities of life.

Of equal interest is the prodigious development of slang peculiar to teen-agers. Valid or not, I have my own suspicions about this phenomenon. I call it that because I believe it to be a relatively recent development. There has, of course, for generations, been localized slang confined to certain schools, just as there has always been private language devised by small groups of children and used among themselves or within the limits of the family, language often shared by the parents. But it is my belief that the emergence of a widespread teen-age slang springs in part from the self-consciousness we have created among that age group. When I say "we," I am thinking primarily of Americans, among whom the cult of youth has reached unprecedented proportions. What other country, for instance, has newspaper columns devoted to the concerns of adolescents?

Another reason for the rapid growth of teen-age slang may be found in the addiction of that age group to the bastardized popular music of our era; they have added to their own private vocabulary the argot of band leaders and those innumerable "singers" who have so distorted the meaning of song. Whether or not my explanation of the origins of our teen-age language is well founded, there can be no doubt that parents are finding it increasingly difficult to understand the speech of their own children.

VIII

Those Four-Letter Words

WHAT WE TEND to forget about four-letter words is that in the Middle Ages and down into the Elizabethan period they were—or so the authorities tell us—taken for granted as a part of accepted speech, and after Gutenberg and Caxton, were also admitted to the printed page. We can therefore assume that nobody was self-conscious about their use.

All of them were of Anglo-Saxon origin, a tongue that favored the short word. Some Anglo-Saxon words, even though monosyllabic, were and still are pleasing to the ear—like *dawn* and *dusk, moon* and *mist, rain* and *wave*. This was not true of the four-letter words which were to become for centuries the pariahs of speech, and which are even now,

after long battles in their behalf, subjects of angry contro-
versy. They range from the merely blunt to the downright
ugly. How much the sound of them had to do with the dis-
favor into which they came is matter for speculation, although I suspect this aspect of them counted for little in
their downward course. What we can say with certainty is
that they became soiled and outcast through association,
just as a man's good name suffers from his known affiliation
with disreputable company. The four-letter words in time
became free to move only in the company of people insensi-
tive to the niceties of speech.

The major offenders among them—those which have only
recently been granted passports to book publication—are six
in number: *piss, fart, shit, fuck, cock* and *cunt.* There are
four others, also Anglo-Saxon in origin, which, in varying degree, have customarily enjoyed greater freedom than the
first group. These are *snot, puke, turd,* and *arse.* Nobody
would call them elegant expressions, but they have not had
to fight for their lives. Three more, two Anglo-Saxon and one
French in origin, complete the list: *dung, spit,* and *rape.*
Dung has always remained a respectable word; it may even
have passed the lips of Queen Victoria; *spit* has led a border-
line existence, and has often had to make way for *expecto-
rate* or *expectoration. Rape,* the one "four-letter word" of
French derivation, has gone scot-free; even the family newspaper gives it the green light.

Our chief concern, however, is with the Big Six. Apparently
there was some uneasiness about their use as early as Chaucer, who died in 1400. He freely wrote *piss* and *fart,* but
for *fuck* he used *swyve,* a word which did not persist. By
Shakespeare's time the four-letter words were definitely in
decline, though some held on; he himself never used all of
them in the text of his plays, whatever may have been his

practice in speech. I do not know how thoroughly Mark Twain explored Elizabethan English before writing *1601*, the "Fireside Conversation at the Court of Queen Elizabeth," which he limited to distribution among his friends, and which even now leads a somewhat subterranean life. In any case, although in that privately printed little book he indulged himself in *fart*, when it came to more potent matters he did not, for example, use the word *cunt*; he referred to "so sweet a nest." Perhaps he feared that his beloved but ever watchful and highly shockable Libby might by chance light upon a copy.

There are things to be said in favor of even the coarsest of the four-letter words. They are forthright and vigorous, and for that reason preferable to the more ponderous and somehow less direct Latinities which, in polite usage, supplanted them. What more than a sort of aseptic merit can be urged in support of *copulate, urinate, defecate, vagina*, and, even though Anglo-Saxon, *break wind?*

Through the centuries *piss* has been granted the largest measure of toleration among the six. It was used without qualm by the creators of the King James Bible, but the translators of the Revised Standard Version saw fit to banish it. Incidentally, one of my reasons for defending it is my fondness for echoic words, and *piss* is surely more expressive and suggestive of the act it stands for than either *pee* or *urinate*, let alone the evasive and roundabout *make water*.

Next in degree of toleration are *fart* and *shit*. I would imagine that most people of both sexes—if not among the Victorians, certainly among ourselves—have employed them now and then. Certainly neither is an attractive word, but one cannot deny that they have a motive force absent in their more respectable synonyms. In connection with them I have long cherished the story of the upright and inhibited

68

judge who, having lost his helpmeet, took some comfort in the sense of liberation that permitted him to give free vent to accumulated intestinal gas. These three words, *piss, shit,* and *fart,* are the only ones, by the way, which have gained admission to our current general dictionaries, although to my surprise I find *shit* omitted from *Webster's New World Dictionary* (College Edition); yet it appears in the *Shorter Oxford English Dictionary,* in spite of the fact that the British taboo on printing (though not on speaking) the four-letter words is in practice more sweeping than our own. All six, it might be added, are included, together with those popular phrases of which they form a part, in the recent Wentworth and Flexner *Dictionary of American Slang.* An amusing footnote to all this is that *fart,* according to *Webster's New World Dictionary of the American Language* was once, in its early days, a euphemism; I have been unable to discover for what.

Perhaps none of the words we have been discussing leads a stranger life than *cock.* It has one of the largest entries in the great *Oxford English Dictionary,* not all of them, of course, concerned with the meaning which placed it on the prohibited list. As a term for the male sexual member, it has probably had wider use than any other substitute for *penis.* It may not be generally realized by many who employ it, that specifically, it refers to that organ when, to use the language of the sex books, it is in "a state of tumescence," or more bluntly, when it is stiff. Shakespeare so used it once, at least, when he wrote in *Henry V* that "Pistol's cock is up." It has variants without this specific connotation, of which *prick* is perhaps the most frequently used, and which if not in number of letters, certainly otherwise belongs in the company of the four-letter words.

It has long been my feeling that of all the six, *cunt* is the most pleasing, and it is hard for me to understand why the sight or sound of it should be offensive. Certainly *vagina* is a depressingly clinical term for such a powerful and attractive magnet, and such blatant vulgarisms as *twat* are truly offensive. I am thinking, of course, of the use of *cunt* in intimate circumstances, as a variant for *pussy;* I am not recommending its indiscriminate use in ordinary conversation, though I do support its appearance in print whenever needed.

We come now to the most debated of these six words, and the one chiefly responsible for the battles over censorship. It is to my mind as well as to my ear the ugliest of the six. Furthermore, though something of an aphrodisiac when used in the bedroom, it is inadequate, I think, to describe the act of love on its higher levels. (It seems odd, by the way, that the Elizabethans, with their great delight in words, at a time when the spoken and written language was burgeoning as it had not done since Chaucer—and without benefit of dictionaries at that—did not extend their venturesome and creative spirit to the enrichment of our poverty-stricken vocabulary for the act of love.)

I am aware that there are many people today who would deny that there are varying levels on which the act of love exists (apart from one person being "better in bed" than another) and who pride themselves on a supposed realism that sees in the sexual act nothing more than a very pleasant and compulsive physical function—no more compulsive than other eliminatory functions, but potentially, at least, by far the pleasantest—indeed, the only one conducive of rapture and transport. That is a point of view I cannot share. I do not deny that for many people the sexual act remains always on a purely animal plane, as it does in the novels of Dreiser, nor that it can so exist under certain circumstances for almost everybody. But for sensitively organized, highly emotional people, it not only can transcend anything else in our sensory experience, but can involve deeply—no doubt more for most women than for men—what for want of a better term we call the spirit. I reserve what we call the soul for those emotional experiences in which the physical element is absent.

It is here that the word *fuck* fails us. It fails us not merely because it grew tainted by low associations, but also because it has no wings; it is an earth-bound word, powerful but not subtle, and too limited in the range of its suggestive capacity. In fact, so far as I know, English does not stand alone in this lack; there is, I believe, no completely satisfactory, all-embracing word for the act of love in any language—an odd failure, it seems to me, in respect to man's most poignant experience, and in view of his fantastic ingenuity, verbal and otherwise. Some may argue that *make love* meets the requirement I find lacking in *fuck,* but the phrase strikes me as too vague, applying as much to mere love-play as it does to the consummate act.

The origins of *fuck* have not been definitely established by the etymologists. Various derivations have been suggested. The most resourceful living student in the field of etymology, so far as English is concerned, Mr. Eric Partridge, has this to say (I spell out his abbreviations) in his etymological dictionary, *Origins:* "That f**k (as British law required him to print it) cannot descend straight from the Latin *futuere* (whence the Old French and French *foutre*) is obvious; that the two words are related is equally obvious. That it cannot derive unaided from the German *ficken,* to strike (in popular speech), to copulate with, is clear; it is no less clear that the English and German words are cognates. To f**k apparently combines the vocalism of *futuere* plus

the consonantism of *ficken*. . . ." Morris Ernst, the lawyer
whose keen intelligence and persuasive talents were largely
responsible for the admission of *Ulysses* to this country
(thus easing the way for the emergence of the four-letter
words into the light of licensed print) has told me of his dis-
covery that *fuck* originally meant to plant: the farmer
fucked his fields. For the validity of this derivation I cannot
vouch, and neither can he, but certainly it would seem to
provide a reasonable explanation for the word's subsequent
development.

Suppose we turn now to consideration of the uses to
which, in book publication at least, our new-found freedom
to employ these words in print has been put. It is one of the
oddities of the taboo against them that there should be, in
the degrees of liberty achieved, distinct gradations, based
upon the form of publication. Easiest to understand is the
narrow latitude the daily press allows itself, and even that
makes little sense when one considers the lurid literature
available to any child at our corner newsstands. It was only
within rather recent years that the newspapers began to exercise their right to use the words *syphilis* and *gonorrhea* in
place of the vaguer *social diseases*. Many papers still do not
permit themselves the use of *whore*, an ancient and an honorable word if ever there was one. The magazines, though
less circumscribed than the newspapers, allow themselves
smaller freedom than books. Except for those addressed to a
select audience, they dare not countenance the four-letter
word. The *Reader's Digest*, for example, with the largest circulation of them all, though often indulging in slightly
bawdy jokes, will not pass the four-letter words—but one
may be sure they are known to almost every reader.

However, in books today, in mounting fashion, the sky's
the limit. All words, so far as propriety goes, now stand

equal in the editor's sight. After the admission here of *Ulysses,* and still more after the unexpurgated *Lady Chatterly's Lover,* the barriers melted away. Both these books were restrained in language compared with some we have had since, notably Henry Miller's *Tropic of Cancer* and *Tropic of Capricorn.* These opened wide the floodgates.

I happen to be allergic, let me say, to the Henry Miller cult. To call him, as more than one well-known writer has done, the greatest living author, is to me poppycock. His serious, messianic passages are muddled and fuzzy to the core, and his equally frequent scatological and amatory pages I find revolting. For a man who protests that he celebrates life, and is praised by his admirers for his love of it, he manages to make the natural affections a fraud, and the act of love one of the most unsavory activities in which human beings indulge. I would not care to live in Henry Miller's world. Though I would defend his right to use whatever words he wants, I deplore the use to which he puts them.

The court decisions that upheld the right of an author, whose intent was not pornographic, to use the words of his choice, and the right of the publisher to print them, was a step toward sanity in a world I regard as far from sane. These decisions were a blow at hypocrisy, which has long seemed to me a more grievous human fault than the so-called seven deadly sins. Hypocrisy is more detestable than pride, anger, envy, gluttony, avarice, sloth and lust, all of which can be more easily condoned. Anger and pride, indeed, can be virtues. Man is the only hypocritical animal, just as he is the only creature, other than the ants, to make massed warfare on his kind. His tears—or some of them—should be substituted for the crocodile's, and that is one reason why he can despise himself so much. He talks one way and acts another, and you can see him at it all over the world.

Any removal of restrictions tends toward an excessive reaction, which is why all revolutions, someone once suggested—I think it was Robert Frost—should stop halfway. There is no doubt that the reaction to the lifting of the ban on the four-letter words in print has been, in this country at least, excessive. That is due in part to the natural law I have referred to, and partly to our national naïveté in matters concerning sex. It is the primitive peoples at one end of the scale, and those whose more developed cultures have the deepest roots, extending far into the past, at the other, who view sex most clearly, and who take it in their stride most easily. For instance, the American Indian on the one hand, and the Chinese or the French and Italians on the other. They can regard sex more humorously than we, as well as more realistically. Certain American Indian tribes have folk tales in which a man's genitals, separated from his body, embark on adventures of their own, and then return. Some of these are very amusing. Similarly, the Katchina dances of the Hopis sometimes include a burlesque of the sexual act —humor of a slapstick kind. We can be humorous about the outer relations between the sexes—their merely social relations—as in our tired jokes at women's expense, but the act itself rarely strikes us as funny, though it sometimes is.

Our naïveté explains in large measure the dreariness of so many sexual scenes in contemporary fiction, and their prevailingly clinical character. When our novelists do not degrade the sexual relation, as many of them do, they are likely to make it boring—and some do both—because of their blow-by-blow descriptions of something nearly all of us can do, but none of us can adequately describe. In much the same fashion they overdo the use of the four-letter words

—or more exactly, one of them. Anybody who has lived among men whose every other word is *fuck* or *fucking* knows how tedious the habit is, and how meaningless it becomes. Does it never occur to writers like James Jones that the effect upon the reader may be similar? In her once-banned novel, *Strange Fruit*, Lillian Smith used *fuck* once or twice with dramatic and telling effect; we need more emulators of her discretion. An artist suggests; he does not pound on your eardrums like a TV commercial. The writer's present free-, dom breeds, too, a certain arrogance. No friend of mine or of yours either, however close, asks us to sit beside him while he performs his natural bodily functions, yet there are writers who invite our presence while these little imperatives of nature are heeded. Why must I suffer in print what I am freed from in life? Why should I be asked, as I recently was in a novel, to attend for two pages while a husband and wife debate whether her pessary should be inserted while she is standing up, or if it would be preferable to perform the operation lying down? What could be of less concern to me than the outcome of their argument?

It is strange, isn't it, that the atmosphere of passion, so faint in the casual, cold-blooded sex of our current fiction, should have been more strongly evoked by such older writers as Flaubert or Tolstoy, to name but two, than it is by our contemporaries, who are in command of so much greater freedom. The intimate relations between a man and a woman are not like the self-reproduction of primitive organisms, and are not to be illumined by microscopic inspection.

A final note on the abuse of the four-letter word: the freedom to print it should, of course, be retained, and the surest way to accomplish that is by the exercise of more discretion, more common sense, and more artistic skill than too many of our novelists display. The responsibility for drowning out the recurrent cries for official censorship lies with the writer, his editor, and his literary agent. Among them, if they so desire, they can banish forever the ghost of Anthony Comstock and at the same time clear the way for a better, broader, and more sensible realism than we are currently offered. For this, I am convinced, innumerable readers would be grateful, and they are by no means confined to your sisters and your aunts. I don't know about your cousins.

I X

The Art of Punctuation

THE ART of punctuation—for such it is—has been going through some queer shenanigans. It is currently better understood and practiced by the British than by ourselves; with us it has become a haphazard, hit or miss affair, when it is not deliberately dismissed as nonessential, or as interfering with the free flow of the stream of consciousness. All three attitudes are about as logical as to throw out the baby with the bath water. It would be idle to deny that there is such a thing as overpunctuation, and it is to the credit of contemporary practice that a plethora of these aids to communication has come to be regarded as cumbersome and irritating. Nobody wants to inhale a comma with every other breath, and the careful writer uses commas as sparingly as possible.

American freewheeling in the matter of punctuation is not surprising, given an elementary and secondary school system in which fundamentals have too often been tossed out the window, plus our deep-seated national antipathy to rules and regulations of any kind. The lapse is the more regrettable because so few writers are able to use words clearly and effectively. Punctuation is an invaluable aid toward insuring clarity and proper emphasis; when its principles are unlearned or ignored, the chances of unintentional obscurity and ineffective structure are greatly increased.

For downgrading of punctuation James Joyce may bear some of the blame. It is likely that *Ulysses* and *Finnegans Wake* have contributed to its disuse. Certainly one can trace to Molly Bloom's soliloquy in *Ulysses* some of the most tiresome and fatiguing pages in modern experimental writing. I maintain that when Joyce dumped the scrambled contents of Molly's consciousness onto the printed page, the remarkable tour de force would have been still more memorable and much less irritating reading if he had made a judicious use of punctuation. He deluded himself into believing that the flow of Molly's mainly scabrous thoughts would be better sustained without those signals which only punctuation can provide. He was, I think, as mistaken as the poet José Garcia Villa in his "comma poems," each of which contain a comma after every word. Villa conceived the notion that the principles of *pointillisme* in painting could be transferred to the art of writing, forgetting completely that one sees a painting as a whole, whereas a poem or any other body of writing must be apprehended piecemeal, no matter

78

how many words a reader is capable of absorbing at one glance.

The anarchic influence of Joyce is easily evident in the muddy flow of too much of the prose written by even such talented writers as Jack Kerouac, whose undeniable gift for fresh observation and statement is almost lost in the riotous jungle created by his freewheeling, breathless construction. Some of his sentences resemble nothing so much as the Mississippi losing itself in the Delta.

Many contemporary poets have practically abandoned punctuation. Some omit it completely; others rely on a wholly unpredictable use of the colon, that otherwise increasingly neglected stepchild of modern punctuation. I have sometimes tried without success to determine for just what purpose the colon was used in many lines of contemporary poetry, and was forced to conclude that the poet had employed it merely as a means of catching his breath. Actually, punctuation did begin as a breath-taking device, and there has long been a division, between those who primarily so regard it and those who support the later view, which insists upon punctuation's function as an integral part of the pattern of a sentence. Incidentally, Fowler, in *Modern English Usage*, has a witty definition of the colon's proper use as "that of delivering the goods that have been invoiced in the preceding words."

If the overpopulation of sentences by commas has, with reason, been curbed, there need be no regret over the decline of the exclamation mark; it has its uses, but they were once much more heavily abused than now. Its overuse constitutes a confession that the writer lacks sufficient skill in his deployment of words to secure the emphasis he seeks. The comma, the semicolon, and the colon appear infrequently in current prose not only because our writing has grown more informal and our sentence structure less elaborate—but also, I fear, because too many writers are uncertain and confused about their proper use.

There are other tendencies afoot over which I should like to sound a note of moderate alarm. One is the growing contempt in which the apostrophe is held. A good many years ago Bernard Shaw declared war on that innocuous little mark. How much this had to do with more recent assaults I don't know, but they increase in number. First they were confined to dropping the apostrophe from *don't* and *can't* and *won't*. Recently I have seen this amputation senselessly extended to contractions like *I'd* and *he'd* and *she'd,* a form of mutilation for which I can see no possible excuse.

Desirable though the movement away from excessive punctuation has been, there is danger that we may presently find ourselves without enough, and that the confusion rising out of the blurred meaning of so many important words, such as *democracy, liberal,* and the like, plus the dismaying spread of gobbledygook, may be heightened because insufficient thought and attention are being given to the art of punctuation. It was Poe who said: "Even where the sense is perfectly clear, a sentence may be deprived of half its force—its spirit, its point—by improper punctuation. For the want of merely a comma, it often occurs that an axiom appears a paradox, or that a sarcasm is converted into a sermonoid."

There is a story about Richard Brinsley Sheridan that points up better than anything else I know the potentialities of punctuation. While the playwright was a member of the British Parliament, he was once called upon to apologize to a fellow member. He rose and said (and I reprint his remark without punctuation): "Mr. Speaker, I said the honorable member was a liar it is true and I am sorry for it," adding that the honorable member could place the punctuation marks where he pleased.

Equally amusing is the instance offered by Mr. William B. Plummer, who informs me that the North Dakota Legislature once passed a law which, in the form in which it was printed, seemed to ban all residents and visitors from sleeping in a hotel. The statute read something like this: "It is hereby declared . . . illegal . . . punishable by . . . for any person to sleep in any restaurant, café, hotel, dining room or any other public eating place." That's what a misplaced comma can do. Mr. Plummer also mentioned the now obsolete English practice of writing contracts and agreements in unpunctuated paragraphs, each paragraph covering one phase of the agreement in its entirety and comprising what—to anyone but an English lawyer—would have been two to twenty sentences. And one recalls that "Lord" Timothy Dexter, the famous eccentric of Newburyport, Massachusetts, wrote a book in which he put all the punctuation marks in an appendix, inviting the reader to place them where he pleased—an innovation that might well be followed, with profit to the reader, by some of our more unconventional or illiterate writers.

By far the most interesting and most significant trend in our punctuational habits is the rapidly mounting use of the quotation mark as a way of qualifying meaning. I am certainly not the first to call attention to this phenomenon; it has been recognized for several years. The interest and significance of the practice derive from the fact that it is so closely associated with our contemporary fuzziness in the use of words. Too many of them, intended to express highly important concepts, have become purely relative in actual meaning. The interpretation to be placed upon them by the reader depends often upon the sense in which they were used by the writer, who, to worsen matters considerably, is frequently at sea as to the precise meaning which he himself wishes them to convey. When, for example, the word "liberal" is enclosed by quotation marks, the implication is clear that the person or idea so referred to is, in the writer's estimation at least, not liberal at all. When "democratic" is similarly written, the hint is obvious that *totalitarian* is actually implied. When you refer to a female as a "lady," you are either implying that she is a woman of dubious respectability, or one with social pretensions to which she has no actual claim.

It would be possible to write an entire page or a complete article in which no noun or verb or adjective was intended to convey the meaning ordinarily associated with it. The practice is, indeed, so insidious that I have seen articles in which such an ultimate was almost achieved. It is difficult to avoid too frequent use of this technique because the conditions which have induced the practice are continually spreading and deepening. Indeed, Joseph Wood Krutch several years ago published an article called "Let's Be Prejudiced," in which, the better to make his points, it was necessary for him to use liberally those betraying quotation marks. The way things are going, it will soon be necessary for typewriter manufacturers to build in a specially reinforced key for the quotation mark.

Few of us, grammarians aside, have given thought to the history of punctuation, however much or little we may know about its principles. What little I know has been derived from *The Pattern of English,* by G. H. Vallins. This, a volume in the Pelican series of Penguin Books, is a history of the developments in the construction of the English prose sentence, and it contains an interesting chapter on the history of English punctuation. Did you know, for example, that in the earliest books printed in English there were but three punctuation marks: a stroke (/), marking off word-groups or phrases; a colon, marking a distinct syntactical break or pause, and a full stop marking either the end of a sentence or a brief pause? Or that the exclamation mark was once known as the "note of admiration," deriving from the old Latin sense of *admire*—wonder? There is a theory that this mark was originally *Io*, the Latin exclamation of joy, written as I, with a small circle underneath, and that the form of I became obscured and the o filled up? Did you know that quotation marks did not appear in English writing until the end of the seventeenth century?

Perhaps because the British take punctuation more seriously than we do, the best books that I have seen on the subject are by English writers. Two of particular value are G. V. Carey's *Mind the Stop* and Eric Partridge's *You Have a Point There*. The second has a separate chapter on American practice.

X

Why Johnny Can't Spell

THE ABILITY to spell, like the gift of mimicry, seems to be not so much acquirable as it is innate. Those of us who are strongly visual-minded, who have no difficulty, for example, in recalling whether a certain passage in a book was encountered on the left- or right-hand page, are likely to be proficient spellers, whether or not we have had much drilling in the matter. Certainly the ability to spell has little to do with intelligence; some of the liveliest minds may be found among men who spell atrociously. So too, some of the most skilled writers seem baffled by the alphabet; Scott Fitzgerald was one, and his friend Hemingway, though not as helpless as Fitzgerald, was frequently unsure.

84

The average level of spelling skill, it seems to me, has definitely declined among Americans during the last few decades. In large measure this has been due to the distaste for disciplines of any kind that has characterized so much of our teaching on the primary and high-school levels. When I attended public school in New York during the late 'nineties, spelling bees, in which all the upper grades participated, in assembly before the entire school, were frequent. They are rare occasions now, and any college teacher of English will tell you how badly words are mangled in the freshman themes he reads. That inability to spell does not end with the college years, will be confirmed by the editors of any publishing house.

As every foreigner who has applied himself to English knows, its spelling far outruns in difficulty that of his native tongue. It is wildly erratic, and almost wholly without logic. One needs the eye of a hawk, the ear of a dog, and the memory of an elephant to make headway against its confusions and inconsistencies. No wonder simplified spelling campaigns have been recurrent for centuries. Of late years, the pleading or angry voice of the spelling reformer has not been so loud in the land; the last real stir of this kind was made when the will of Bernard Shaw disclosed that he had left much of his large fortune to the cause of furthering a radical revision of written English, for "simplified spelling" is too mild a term for the changes he had in mind. What he wanted was a new alphabet, and just recently we had our first opportunity to see what it looked like. For my own part, I am happy that its adoption on any large scale seems most unlikely. Only by the inclusion of additional vowels and consonants, he had contended, could the absurdities and waste of our present spelling be removed. As nearly as possible, he wanted English written as it is spoken: a worthy objective, but by the means proposed, hardly conducive to raising an army of devoted adherents.

Ever since the late sixteenth century there have been concerted efforts not only to bring writing closer to speech, but to bring order out of varying degrees of chaos. The chaos was greatest in the Elizabethan Age, when the language, like the world's horizons, was growing at exhilarating speed, and the word-mint was working faster than a national treasury lashed by inflation. So great was the ferment that a determined effort toward standardization seemed imperative, and because of this situation there was, in the late sixteenth and early seventeenth centuries, a succession of influential spelling reformers whose names are known today only to lexicographers. Through their efforts a marked degree of simplification and uniformity became evident in the later decades of the seventeenth century.

The greater part of these changes had to do with the omission of unnecessary letters. As anyone interested in ciphers knows, "e" is the most frequently used letter in English, but its predominance is less marked today than it was in Chaucerian and Elizabethan writing. The Elizabethans discarded some of Chaucer's omnipresent "e's," but like him they placed many of them at the ends of words, partly but not entirely because they had been sounded in the speech of Chaucer's time. For some there had been no reason whatever. These "e" endings have rarely been used since the end of the seventeenth century—such spellings as *runne, halfe, houre, betweene.* The Elizabethans were also more lavish than we with the use of consonants; they wrote *sette* and *dimme* and *sunne.* Some of the unnecessary letters they used, like "k" after "c" in words such as *publick* and *almanack,* persisted longer, and are frequently found in eighteenth-century writing.

86

Another spelling upheaval occurred when the American colonies began to acquire a native idiom. It is seldom remembered now that among Benjamin Franklin's widely varied interests was a zealous concern for spelling reform. Like Bernard Shaw, he was all out for a phonetically written English, and in 1768 published his *Scheme for a New Alphabet and a Reformed Mode of Spelling*. The arguments he put forth were later to influence Noah Webster. Webster held to certain reservations, yet his American Dictionary of 1828, although less radical than some of his earlier recommendations, relies more on phonetic principles than do the dictionaries in use today.

The most recent wave of wide popular interest and participation in spelling reform came nearly sixty years ago, in 1906, when Theodore Roosevelt, with customary vehemence, gave his support to the reformers. Scholars like Thomas Lounsbury and Brander Matthews were advocating a rather moderate program involving three hundred words which they believed should be more simply spelled. Their proposals included such new spellings as *thru* and *thoroly*. Although one still encounters them occasionally, the movement has of late made no perceptible headway.

Never slow to act on his convictions, Roosevelt wrote during his Presidency to the director of the Government Printing Office, requesting him to use this simplified spelling in all government publications, including Presidential messages. He followed this with an official order, or, as we would now say, for what good purpose I have yet to determine, *directive*. But the Supreme Court disregarded his recommendations, and the House, after receiving his 1906 message, written in the new orthography, passed a resolution forbidding any departure from standard spelling in any publications authorized by law. The press of the period had a lot of fun with the new spelling while the furor lasted.

As a matter of fact, reformers or no reformers, a slow but steady change occurs in our spelling, just as the meanings of words so often suffer a sea change. Words, or more accurately those who employ them, seem to defy the preferences of any self-appointed group, and choose to obey the deep-running tide of popular usage. So, too, with the practice of capitalizing the initial letter of certain common nouns. This was general practice as late as the eighteenth century, and was continued by some writers—Carlyle and Emerson, for example—well into the nineteenth. It has almost disappeared in our own, except for its aid in obtaining humorous effects in such work as George Ade's *Fables in Slang*. Today, even Nature, the most persistent of these capitalizations aside from the Deity, God, certain other ecclesiastical terms, and those involving government, is more often than not begun in lower case.

The British and ourselves, of course, more or less resolutely retain some differences in spelling. They still cling to *humour* and *honour*—as Shaw clung to *shew* for *show*—but we long ago discarded the "u." One observes among the British a growing tendency to adopt the American variant in some instances, just as in recent years they have accepted for their own use (though not without occasional cries of anguish and concern) many American words and phrases which have either struck their fancy or burrowed a way into popular use by constant repetition in imported American movies. On the other hand, some Americans seem to find more glamor in *glamour*, and the rabid Anglophiles among us display a hankering for such British terms as *cinema*, and such British spellings as *cheque*. For my own part, I do not crave to say *cravat* for *tie*, *braces* for *suspenders*, *boots* for *shoes*, *vest* for *undershirt*, or *lift* for *elevator*. In general it may be said that the trade balance both in words and spelling has grown markedly in our favor.

To return briefly to the fortunes of spelling reform: my guess is that it will continue to be gradual, as it nearly always has been. High on my own list for alteration are such words as *dialogue* and *catalogue*. What possible justification is there for retaining the last two letters? And similarly, I think Mr. Coolidge might in all logic have announced, "I do not *chuse* to run." As a harmless way of inducing sleep, I suggest listing such changes for the better as may occur to you.

As a matter of fact, a good case can be made for a measure of anarchy in spelling. Indeed, it was once briefly made by Havelock Ellis, in that rich book *The Dance of Life*. "Even when," he wrote, "we leave out of consideration the great historical tradition of variety in this matter, it is doubtful . . . whether the advantages of encouraging everyone to spell like his fellows overbalance the advantages of encouraging everyone to spell unlike his fellows. When I was a teacher in the Australian Bush, I derived far less enjoyment from the more or less 'correctly' spelt exercises of my pupils than from the occasional notes I received from their parents who, never having been taught to spell, were able to spell in the grand manner. We are wilfully throwing away an endless source of delight. . . ."

XI

Embattled Words of the Bible

FEW DISCUSSIONS bearing on the choice of words produce as heated comment as those concerning the relative merits of the King James Version of the Bible and the modern translations which have followed it. If anything in our literary past is held sacrosanct—and I do not mean in the religious sense of holy—it is the King James version. Merely to lay hands on it with a view to alteration raises the hackles of thousands of readers, even though they may not have turned its pages in many years. They are deaf or indifferent to the protestations of Scriptural scholars who insist that, in addition to normal changes in the meaning of words, linguistic research has revealed gross inaccuracies in the work of the seventeenth-century translators, however magnificent as prose their rendering was.

The champions of the newer versions, on the other hand, maintain that a proper understanding of many passages is impossible without the aid of the revised text. Common sense, of course, dictates that we value each version for what it gives. No sensible and sensitive person wants to forego the majesty of the Jacobean text, by which nearly four centuries of our literature have been impregnated, nor, if he is concerned with accurate meaning as much as he is delighted by glorious sound, will he want to dispense with the modern findings. After all, eighty-odd years have elapsed since publication of the first Revised Version and ten since the completion of the second. During those years textual criticism continued to advance. Even as the first Revised Version was deemed necessary in view of the changes in English and the better understanding of the original manuscripts which had come about since 1611, so have similar alterations occurred since 1881.

Even though the thought and language of the Bible is no longer as deeply woven into the fabric of American life as it was in the days when daily readings from Scripture were standard practice in so many American homes, emotional reaction does not slacken as successive new renderings appear. Partly this is due to the fact that the differences between the old and later versions were not sufficiently explained. They were briefly referred to in the preface to the Revised Standard Version which was published in 1953, but except for readers of the religious journals there was not available any detailed consideration of them until 1960. Then Ronald Bridges, former President of the Pacific School of Religion, and Luther A. Weigle, Dean and Sterling Professor Emeritus of the Yale University Divinity

School, himself a translator of the Bible, published *The Bible Word Book*, devoted to more than eight hundred words and phrases which were used in the King James Version, but which have either become obsolete or archaic, or have changed in meaning. Though similar volumes were compiled in 1866 and again in 1884, the intervening changes have been so many that a new treatment of the subject was needed. The index lists some eighteen hundred additional words that do not appear in the KJV, but that are used in the revised versions or other modern translations.

Messrs. Bridges and Weigle have written brief histories of the words that have disappeared from use or have altered in meaning, in each case defining carefully the sense in which they were used, not only by King James's scholars, but often by earlier and later translators. Some of the entries, aside from their value as aids to the understanding of Scripture, are fascinating examples of the often extraordinary life histories of words.

Take such a common word as *conversation.* In the KJV it invariably refers to conduct, behavior, or manner of life. Never is it used in the sense it has today. One example of how misleading the KJV's use of this word can be to the uninformed reader is contained in the injunction to the Christian wives of unbelieving husbands, as set down in the non-Pauline Epistles. It reads: "Likewise, ye wives, be in subjection to your own husbands; that, if any obey not the word, they may also without the word be won by the conversation of their wives; While they behold your chaste conversation coupled with fear." Now, as *The Bible Word Book* observes, this sentence conveys the impression that "these wives are to talk their husbands into becoming Christians, though it seems strange that husbands are to *behold* the conversation rather than *listen* to it, and one can only wonder what being coupled with fear has to do with it. But there is no word in the Greek for *coupled,* and no justification for dragging it in; the word *fear* stands for the reverent fear of God which is the mark of a good Christian; and the *conversation* of these women is their behavior."

In the recent Revised Standard Version, the passage is thus altered: "Likewise you wives, be submissive to your husbands, so that some, though they do not obey the word, may be won without a word by the behavior of their wives, when they see your reverent and chaste behavior." The *New English Bible* offers this better version: "In the same way you women must accept the authority of your husbands, so that if there are any of them who disbelieve the Gospel they may be won over, without a word being said, by observing the chaste and reverent behavior of their wives."

Consider that equally familiar but much more difficult word, *love.* Though I had some Greek in college, most of it, to my shame, has gone with the wind, and so I rely on Messrs. Bridges and Weigle for the information that there are three Greek words for *love: eros,* which refers to sexual love, and does not appear in the New Testament; *philia,* which denotes friendship, and occurs only twenty-six times; and then *agape,* which is used more than a hundred times in the New Testament. Now in the KJV a strange thing has happened to this noun. Except for two cases where its plural is used in the sense of love feasts, there remain one hundred twelve occurrences, of which eighty-five are translated as *love,* and twenty-six as *charity.* Tyndale, whose translation preceded the KJV, always translated *agape* as *love.* When rebuked by Sir Thomas More, who wished to retain the Latin-derived and ecclesiastically sanctioned word *charity,* Tyndale replied that "*charity* is not known English, in that sense which *agape* requireth," pointing out that in common usage it meant either alms-giving or patience and mercy in the judgment of others.

The modern translations, in the opinion of Messrs. Bridges and Weigle, "give a surer undergirding to the basic Christian doctrine of God and man than the K.J. The basic principle and ultimate motive of both the Christian gospel and the Christian ethic is love. God is love, and we love because He first loved us. In the translation of *agape*, we are dealing not with a mere exhortation to feeling and action, or even with a statement of human duty, but with the ultimate grounding of human duty and destiny in the very nature and eternal purpose of God. Whatever would tend to separate human love from divine love, or to weaken the essential connection between the Christian ethic and the Christian gospel, is wrong. Yet that is just what the K. J. does, in those twenty-six cases which it tears out of the total fabric of the New Testament teaching."

Consider also the words *admire* and *admiration*. They were used in the seventeenth century to denote wonder or astonishment. The matter of praise or approval was not involved. Thomas Fuller, writing in 1639, said of Mohammedanism that it was "admirable how that senseless religion should gain so much ground on Christianity." He meant, of course, merely that the fact was amazing. And so, when the writer of Revelation, as translated in the KJV, expressed "great admiration" for the woman arrayed in scarlet, "drunken with the blood of the saints and the blood of the martyrs of Jesus," he was simply declaring his amazement. In the RSV his reaction becomes: "when I saw her, I wondered with a great wonder."

What could be more puzzling and more open to misinterpretation than the Biblical phrase, "God is no respecter of persons"? Yet this same idea is repeated in one form or another in a dozen passages of the Old and New Testaments. The meaning becomes clear when one learns that the Greek word translated as "respecter of persons" means "acceptor of the face"—that is, acceptors of the mask an actor wore or the character he assumed. For the translators of the KJV the English word *person* was still close to this meaning, as derived from the Latin *persona,* meaning mask. "It referred," says Mr. Weigle, "to the outward appearance or circumstances of men—to physical presence, dress, wealth, position—rather than to intrinsic worth or to the inner springs of conscious, self-determining being. This text and others using similar words mean that God does not regard mere externals." In the RSV we accordingly have "God shows no partiality," which is a return to Tyndale's translation, "God is not partial."

How many readers have wondered what St. Paul meant when he said, according to the KJV, that "It is better to marry than burn"? The word *burn* is ambiguous until we know that it was a translation of a Greek word more adequately represented in the revised version as "aflame with passion." Not a few readers, one suspects, have shared the supposition of the critic who had always thought the word meant "to burn in hell."

Naturally, considering the waywardness with which words frequently conduct themselves, the language of the KJV offers many instances of words which have either come to stand for worse things than they were, in the seventeenth century, intended to convey, or else have risen in the world to connote something better than they once conveyed. *Base,* in Jacobean times, did not have the evil meaning which we now attach to it. It meant simply, *lowly* or *humble.* The same was true of *vile,* so that in the revised version "our vile body" becomes "our lowly body."

95

Nowadays, when we say of a man that he is "high-minded," we mean to convey that his principles are high, but the seventeenth-century writer used the word in the sense of *proud* or *haughty*. (I am reminded of a Negro maid who exclaimed, when she saw my wife's cat picking its way along the top of a tall bookcase, "You shore is a mighty high-minded cat!") *Naughty* and *naughtiness*, too, have shifted from their former meanings. We use them now for the small misdeeds of children, but for the KJ writers, *naughtiness* was downright wickedness, and the *naughty* figs of Jeremiah's vision were figs so bad they could not be eaten.

Even these few instances are enough to show the need there was for new translations of the Bible. There were, of course, other reasons besides the changes in the meanings of specific words; the greatly enlarged scope of Scriptural knowledge demanded a fresh approach. Many persons will prefer to read certain favorite passages in the version which has meant so much to so many generations of men, but it can no longer stand alone.

Nevertheless, criticism of the new versions has frequently been severe—not on the grounds of scholarship, but on those of style. In too many instances the poetry and the solemn music of the KJV have vanished. The harshest condemnations have been made, and rightly so, I think, in the case of the *New English Bible*. One reviewer wittily characterized it in the caption for his review as "Water in the Wine." One of the severest lacings it received was at the hands of Robert Graves, who found it verbose, often unclear and totally undistinguished in style. Another reviewer, William Harlan Hale, commented that it had been phrased by a group of men with "a tin ear." He thought its English on a par with "the jargon of official hand-out writers and lower-echelon bureaucrats." It sounded to him like George Orwell's Newspeak. Perhaps the most spirited defense of it was made by Gilbert Highet, who, in answer to expected complaints that it "lacks the poetry, even the magic of the old," observed that "the traditional versions of the New Testament (the translation of the Old Testament is still to come) often over-elaborated the original, made it sound nobler in English than it is in the Greek." This view carried considerable weight in view of Mr. Highet's standing as a scholar.

Personally I do not care for the NEB. I have no doubt that in many instances it has struck closer to the precise meaning of the Greek original, and that as a scholarly effort it is commendable, but tang, or even flavor, is missing. I find it a wishy-washy example of current English, and I wait with trepidation for the NEB's rendering of the great Old Testament passages in the KJV. Will it repeat, or even worsen such a pointless change in the Twenty-third Psalm as was made by the RSV, when "thou annointest my head with oil, my cup runneth over," was altered to read, "my cup overflows"?

XII

Some Words to Think About

THERE ARE many words worth careful thought in this age of foggy meanings, sloppy use, and deeply divided attitudes. Chiefly they are words that stand for concepts, whether political, economic, or artistic. We have now been long aware that *democracy* takes its color from its environment, that *progress* may not mean to you what it does to John Doe, that *realism* connotes one thing to this writer and another to his fellow, and that *escape,* as applied to literature, may be variously interpreted.

Two allied words, the distinction between which I have often thought about and tried to fix upon, are *talent* and *genius.* The latter is, I think, one of the most imprecisely used words in the language, and it is that because so few people have made the effort to determine exactly what they mean by it. *Talent* is much easier to define, and less often mistakenly applied. Any group of people engaged in conversation would readily agree upon a definition of *talent* acceptable to them all, but agreement upon the qualities that constitute *genius* would be difficult to reach.

No two words in English are more closely linked by long association and their repeated use in contrast. Because they are so familiar, almost as much a part of our habitual vocabulary as *day* and *night,* they are commonly used with insufficient understanding of why we employ one in preference to the other.

Suppose we open this discussion by consulting the dictionary. In Webster's *New World Dictionary,* which I like for ordinary use because of its prevailing precision of definition, I find this entry under *talent:* "any natural ability or power; natural endowment"; also, "a special, superior ability in an art, mechanics, learning, etc." Then, under synonyms, I find these distinctions made between talent and genius: "talent implies a native ability for a specific pursuit and connotes either that it is or can be cultivated by the one possessing it." That, it seems to me, is admirably clear and comprehensive. Bypassing *gift, aptitude, faculty,* and *knack* as not essential to this discussion, we come to *genius* and are told that it "implies an inborn mental endowment, specifically of a creative or inventive kind in the arts and sciences, that is exceptional or phenomenal." Now this is indisputably descriptive of genius, yet I do not regard it as a satisfying definition. It does not tell us what genius actually is. How are we to distinguish it from talent? Talent also is an inborn mental endowment, exhibited in the arts and sciences, and it may be exceptional or even phenomenal.

A closer approach to the distinguishing qualities of genius is made by the great *Oxford English Dictionary* when it states that the word has come to denote "that particular kind of intellectual power which has the appearance of proceeding from a supernatural inspiration or possession, and which seems to arrive at its results in an inexplicable and miraculous manner." Genius, the *O.E.D.* goes on to say, "achieves its results by instinctive perception and spontaneous activity, rather than by processes which admit of being distinctly analyzed."

But there is still more to be said by way of clarification, as we shall presently see. Many men have attempted to isolate the qualities by which genius may be recognized, among them some whom we would characterize as geniuses themselves. Edison, whose title to the term is surely beyond question, said that "Genius is one per cent inspiration and 99 per cent perspiration." Though this describes rather than defines, it has a certain perception, but we need not, of course, take Edison's words too seriously. In the first place, he was a modest man and a prodigious worker (which not all geniuses are, notably Coleridge); secondly, he was, we may be sure, forgivably pleased by the apposition of inspiration and perspiration.

Helvetius said much the same thing: "Genius is nothing but continued attention," and Hogarth declared, "I know no such thing as genius; it is nothing but labor and diligence." I think his contemporary, Sir Joshua Reynolds, hit closer to the mark when he observed: "Genius is supposed to be a power of producing excellencies which are out of the reach of the rules of art; a power which no precepts can teach, and which no industry can acquire." Ruskin got near the heart of the matter when he said that genius is only "a superior power of seeing." So did Coleridge when he wrote, "To carry the feelings of childhood into the powers of manhood, to combine the child's sense of wonder and novelty with the appearance which every day for years has rendered familiar, that is the character and privilege of genius, and one of the marks which distinguish it from talent."

But I have kept you waiting long enough for the definition that pleases and satisfies me most. It is the conclusion reached by William James in his masterly *Principles of Psychology*. I have only one reservation about it, which is that its truth is more readily perceived in connection with science than with the arts. I believe it holds true for them also, but its application there may not be as quickly grasped.

What James wrote about genius is essentially akin to Hogarth's emphasis on continued attention, and Ruskin's on the power of seeing. But it goes beyond their statements in its reasoned approach and its more specific quality. "Some people," wrote James, "are far more sensitive to resemblances, and far more ready to point out wherein they consist, than others are. They are the wits, the poets, the inventors, the scientific men, the practical geniuses." This faculty for perceiving analogies, he believed, is the dominant factor in genius of every order. To be more specific, consider Newton and Darwin. "The flash of similarity," James pointed out, "between an apple and the moon, between the rivalry for food in nature and the rivalry for man's selection, was too recondite to have occurred to any but exceptional minds. Genius, then, . . . is identical with the possession of similar association to an extreme degree." For demonstration of this principle, James credited the nineteenth-century Scottish psychologist, Alexander Bain.

One of the distinctions drawn between talent and genius is on the score of prodigality; we tend to think of genius as extraordinarily fertile, and more readily conceive of talent as flowing in a thinner stream. Yet talent can be hugely productive and genius can appear only in flashes. We speak of something as being "a stroke of genius"; what we usually have in mind is an exhibition of uncommon skill, but is not that a performance of which talent is capable?

If there is a real distinction in this matter of prodigality, wherein does it lie? Nothing more sensible has been written on the subject than what Somerset Maugham had to say in *The Summing Up*. "I do not believe," he wrote, "that genius is an entirely different thing than talent. I am not even sure that it depends on any great difference in the artist's natural gifts. For example, I do not think that Cervantes had an exceptional gift for writing; few people would deny his genius. Nor would it be easy in English literature to find a poet with a happier gift than Herrick, and yet no one would claim that he had more than a delightful talent. It seems to me that what makes genius is the combination of natural gifts with an idiosyncracy that enables its possessor to see the world personally in the highest degree and yet with such catholicity that his appeal is not to this type of man or that type, but to all men."

Emerson expressed a similar thought when he said: "In every work of genius we recognize our own rejected thoughts; they come back to us with a certain alienated majesty."

Maugham went on to say that even when we are unable to grasp the exact significance of what the genius is communicating, we feel that it is important. "He is supremely normal. By a happy accident of nature seeing life with immense vivacity, as it were at concert pitch, he sees it with its infinite diversity, in the healthy way that mankind at large sees it. In Matthew Arnold's phrase he sees it steadily and sees it whole."

This, it seems to me, is a valid distinction, resting on a firmer base than one where the line is drawn on the grounds of artistry. Perhaps the easiest way of testing its worth is to apply it to some of the great novelists. Tolstoy, for example, is not as subtle an artist as Turgenev or Henry James; his language has less distinction, yet it is he, not the other two, because of the breadth of his appeal, to whom we unhesitatingly give the title of genius. Dickens is full of crudities, yet there is no English novelist whom we would more readily place in a category above talent.

To no other American writer, I suppose, has the term genius been applied as frequently as to Poe. Yet, within the compass of Maugham's distinction he must be denied that rating, for he does not speak to all men, nor does he see life in all its diversity. It is interesting, incidentally, to recall Poe's own words on the subject of genius: "What the world calls genius is the state of mental disease arising from the undue predominance of some one of the faculties. The works of such genius are never sound in themselves, and in especial, always betray the general mental insanity."

Maugham observes, perhaps with his customary capacity to see himself detachedly and clearly, that under the heading of talent, and he includes himself, must come the names of many whose work has uncommon merit. "When you think it has produced such novels as *Le Rouge et le Noir,* such poems as *The Shropshire Lad,* such paintings as those of Watteau, there is not much to be ashamed of."

In addition to the universality which distinguishes it, there is another characteristic of genius which Maugham might have noted. Dr. Johnson, with his usual sharp perception and prevailing common sense, described it when he wrote, "The true genius is a mind of large general powers accidentally determined to some particular direction"—a much truer observation than his remark to the effect that "genius is nothing more than knowing the use of tools." One thinks in this connection of such minds as Goethe's, who, although he did, in addition to his literary work, contribute something to the scientific knowledge of his time, might well be numbered among the world's great scientists instead of one of its great poets, had he not been impelled to divide his energies.

Several years ago, I listened to further confirmation of the truth of Dr. Johnson's observation, when Professor Marston Morse of the School for Advanced Studies at Princeton read a remarkable paper on the affinity between the higher mathematics and the creative arts. Both, he convincingly demonstrated, arrive at their conclusions (in the case of mathematics) and their expression of thought or feeling (in the case of the arts) by processes which are fundamentally similar. For both the mathematician or other scientist, as for the artist, the perception of those analogies to which William James called attention, is achieved by an unexplainable leap of intellect, like the bridging of space by an electric spark.

If one grants the kinship between the creative process as it operates in science and as it does in art, let us see how James applies the principle of analogy, of association, to its operation in literature. He offers as one instance this passage from Homer: "Ulysses, too, spied round the house to see if any man were still alive and hiding, trying to get away from gloomy death. He found them all fallen in the blood and dirt, and in such number as the fish which the fishermen to the low shore, out of the foaming sea, drag with their meshy nets. These all, sick for the ocean water, are strewn around the sands, while the blazing sun takes their life from them. So there the suitors lay strewn round on one another."

James wrote of what has been said of Shakespeare—that

he possessed more intellectual power than anyone who ever lived—that if this meant the power to pass from the given premises to congruous conclusions, "it is no doubt true." In support of this statement, he went on to say, "The abrupt transitions in Shakespeare's thought astonish the reader by their unexpectedness no less than they delight him by their fitness. . . ."

This capacity shared by Homer and Shakespeare is the indubitable mark of genius. There is much more, then, behind the word *genius* than is to be confined within the limits of a dictionary definition.

XIII

Words of Tomorrow

ONE OF the oldest axioms about language is that it is not static. All civilized tongues—and possibly those of primitive peoples—are in continual flux, and this is more true, perhaps, of our own than of any other. I daresay that English has suffered more sea changes since the fourteenth century, when it began to assume a character recognizable to us now, than French, Spanish, Italian, German, or Russian. Nowhere have these changes been as constant or as pronounced as in the United States. English on its home grounds has altered much, of course, but not as markedly as here, where it separated itself sufficiently from parental usage for H. L. Mencken to be emboldened to issue a declaration of verbal independence. You may recall that he wrote three stout and fascinating volumes on what he chose to call "the American Language."

What Mencken, in his proselyting zeal, did not foresee was that British and American English, both written and spoken, would draw closer together. This rapprochement has been in progress since World War I, following several decades in which American writers were forging a native style, more closely approximating the differences which distinguished our speech from that of the mother country. The source for this development has been too commonly attributed to Mark Twain, who, though he did more to advance it than Thoreau (slower in reaching a wide public), was by no means the pioneer that Hemingway called him in stating flatly that "American writing begins with Mark Twain." Not only did Thoreau precede Twain in arriving at a native style; so, too, at times did his mentor Emerson. And earlier still, even though Benjamin Franklin studied Addison and Steele, there are definite traces in his autobiography of an emerging native idiom. Its growth was checked by the subservience of so many American writers, especially those of the genteel school, to British models. This literary kowtowing was still rife in the mid and late Victorian periods, but the seeds of rebellion had already been sown before Mark Twain first put pen to paper.

If, prior to Mark Twain (who did not achieve a wide readership until the late eighteen sixties), we were prevailingly influenced by English models—and continued to be even past the turn of the century—the balance of power began perceptibly to shift with the coming of World War I. The influence of our own speech and writing on the British began then, too, and has proceeded since at an increasingly accelerated pace. This type of coexistence, though a matter of indifference to us, has not been universally welcomed by our British brethren. Occasional angry voices are lifted in the *Times* of London and other publications, protesting that this linguistic miscegenation must be halted at once.

The march of language, forward or backward, cannot be halted. Although that march is speedier and more insistent in matters of speech, it is no less perceptible on the printed page. Though Hollywood may have set the pace for British borrowings from us, the periodical press, though not books, has not been too far behind. The *Times* of London may remain adamant, but some other English papers have not been above a flattering interest in American newspaper style. And if Sydney Smith could once—and not wholly without justification—inquire, "Who reads an American book?" no literate Englishman today would raise such a question. Even *Punch* would laugh at him.

The gulf between us and the British in manner of speech, choice of words, and even of cadence, grows steadily narrower. The once famous, and to our ears unintelligible, Oxford drawl has almost passed from hearing, and the speech of the cultivated Britisher and the cultivated American approximate each other more and more. The differences, for example, between F.D.R.'s and Churchill's speech were slight. Where we still differ widely—and this much to our discredit—is in the rhythms of speech. Ours holds to an almost deadly monotone; the British manner of running up and down the scale, when not exaggerated, is far more pleasing and far less boring to the ear. (There we have one reason why Americans flock to British plays; their actors are better trained in speech, as they also are in the acting art. This difference, I think, is indisputable.) We are still baffled, though, by the speech of the Cockney; more so, perhaps, than an Englishman is by the Brooklyn or Bronx accent.

The writing differences remain greater, and some of these also are not to our credit. We need yield the British nothing on the score of vitality, but on that of regard for the language, and knowledge of its grammar and punctuation, we must yield them much. The sorry fact is that the English schools still place a proper emphasis on fundamentals in language training; ours, for too long a time, permitted madcap theories to produce a generation or two of near-illiterates. I find the general level of British writing, both in periodicals and books, superior to ours in mastery of fundamental skills. As a rule, its sentences are better constructed, freer from grammatical error, and better punctuated. We may match or surpass the British in content, but in style—and mind you I am speaking only of the average writer—we remain inferior. When one comes to a Hemingway, a Faulkner (at his best), a Frost, a Thurber, or an E. B. White (all but one of whom, I sadly note, are dead), my generalization has no point. But in the case of the average American first novel as opposed to the average British, I am confident it has a great deal.

My concern with the words of tomorrow is by no means limited to such further verbal fellowship as may come about between the British and ourselves. (The more palsy-walsy we become in this respect, the greater the likelihood, I fear, that other and more important differences may arise —on the theory that the more easily people communicate, the easier it is for them to separate: Adams' Law of Diminishing Returns.) If I seem to contradict certain observations made in the opening chapter, let me reassure myself by repeating Emerson to the effect that "a foolish consistency is the hobgoblin of little minds."

I am thinking also of such current menaces as the speed-reading craze. The proponents of this fiendish effort to convert the human reader into some kind of IBM computer put a very low value on quality in words and the manner in which they are assembled. They will dispute this charge, of course, but I do not think they can disprove it. Words as they wish us to see them become like so many nickels, dimes, quarters or cartwheels which you might drop in the maw of a one-arm bandit in the expectation of hitting the jackpot. One quarter or cartwheel serves this purpose just as well as another.

It is not my intention or my wish to throw their entire effort into the ashcan. Their methods, which they guarantee will make it possible for you to consume several pages of print in the time it now takes you to consume but one, may serve very well for certain menial purposes; they will enable you to swallow whole a *Reader's Digest* article which you now nibble at piecemeal; they will assist you to get through your favorite newspaper (provided it is not the New York *Times*) before you have finished your morning grapefruit; they will make it possible for you to cut in half the time you now spend on the latest whodunit—but I will bet dollars to doughnuts that they will not increase your appreciation of any first-rate writer, whether he be poet, novelist, or essayist. You will, in fact, lose the greater part of what you were able to get before, even if your eyes formerly had the speed of a moving tortoise. It isn't humanly possible to take in a fat paragraph at a glance, and beyond absorbing the general sense of it, receive any adequate notion of its structure, its music, if any, its shadings of meaning or its subtleties of thought. Reading is not a one-way street; you get from it in proportion to what you give, and if all you give is a rapid-fire runover, what can you expect for your money? Try reading the Twenty-third Psalm at a glance. That is not perhaps a satisfactory example, for the words are too well known, even today, although I would wager there are fifteen million teen-agers who couldn't distinguish it from a TV commercial. I know there are thousands of bright, even brilliant, and reasonably well-read teen-agers, for I have listened to some of them; I am talking, however, in terms of national averages.

Not many years ago the New York *Times* made a painstaking survey of the geographical knowledge possessed by American schoolchildren, including those of high-school and college age. The findings were nothing less than appalling —at least to anybody in my own age group, for we had been drilled in geography at a tender age, as we had been also in handwriting, spelling, grammar, punctuation, and what have you, in which the unfolding mind needs drilling. Far too many of these youngsters, the *Times* survey proved, were hazy, if not totally ignorant regarding the simplest facts about the geography of their own country.

Only the other day I was astounded when my eldest granddaughter, a bright teen-ager (as well as a beautiful one) looked down the street on which I live and asked what river that was, a hundred yards away. It happens to be the East River (and she should have known, of course, that actually it is not a river at all, but a channel). Pointing west, up Fifty-seventh Street, I asked her what other river lay at its end; she didn't know the Hudson was there. I went to public grammar school in New York in the late eighteen-nineties and early nineteen hundreds, and I doubt whether any child there would have been unable to identify, both in name and place, the East and Hudson rivers, between which they lived. My granddaughter has an excellent IQ and is a voracious reader—and not of the comics—yet, on these matters, due to our educational collapse, she was lamentably ignorant. Small wonder, then, that Admiral Rickover blew his top. The

Soviets, however repugnant their system is to us, have had the sense to hold to the old discipline in education. We had better take note, and soon.

To continue for a moment with this digression, there has developed in this country during recent years an astounding proliferation of books devoted to the so-called needs of teenagers. This is a publishing racket, pure and simple. Teen-agers need teen-age books like they need a hole in the head. What they need are books that make them stretch their minds; it doesn't matter if they do not understand all of what they read. They should feed on books addressed to adults, as their grandparents did; not that we didn't have our own writers—Henty and Stratemeyer, Edward Ellis and Oliver Optic and Horatio Alger, not to speak of the dime novels we read in seclusion. But these were not our only fare; we read much more besides if we had the free run of a library. We were not encouraged to look upon ourselves as a separate and special group, with special needs; we were presently to become men and women, and we were not fed pap, like a predigested breakfast food. Teen-agers today are treated as if they were an underprivileged minority, and their parents stand abashedly in awe of them. If Johnny wants a car, he must have it, even if he doesn't know that the United States lies between the Atlantic and Pacific Oceans. And his sister must have the latest hair-do, even if she doesn't know that Betsy Ross designed the first American flag.

Speedreading is not the only menace that threatens the words of tomorrow. We pride ourselves on our bluntness of speech, on our distaste for old-fashioned oratory—or any oratory, for that matter—and yet we coin as many or more nice Nellieisms as the Victorians, with their *limbs* for *legs*. They were, as a matter of fact, more honest in some respects, for they simply declined to use the words they thought offensive, instead of devising pale substitutes for them, as we so often do. I say we; what I really mean is that these Uriah Heepish words are foisted on us by the sociologists, the bureaucrats, and other dangerous elements in our society.

One phrase now much in the news, which I would like to see cast into outer darkness, is "senior citizens." This euphemism for the elderly or downright old is almost as offensive as "funeral home." Whoever concocted it—and the originators of these minor monstrosities somehow always remain anonymous—should be baked in oil and then served as a soufflé in the hell he will sometime inhabit. There will, of course, be a special corner of the infernal regions reserved for the Madison Avenue luminary who thought up "Get that kid stuff out of your hair"; he will be afflicted forever with an itching scalp. As for those smirking dolls who lovingly caress their own skins while promoting the last thing in lotions, they will suffer the tortures of perpetual acne.

The words of tomorrow, as foreshadowed in the recent controversial new edition of the Merriam Webster, will of course include a host of technological terms as yet unborn. They will, I predict, be increasingly abstruse and increasingly polysyllabic. Everybody, if Mr. Kennedy has his way about shooting for the moon, will feel obliged to learn them. The question remains: What will we do with them after they have been acquired? Just as we may ask ourselves: What will we do with the moon after we have set foot on it?

The Scientists (now so important in our lives that I feel compelled to capitalize the word for them as we capitalize the Deity) have announced that Venus, once just a lovely apparition in the early evening and morning skies has a prevailing temperature of 800° Fahrenheit, and that its inhabitants, if any, look upward into a smog thicker than any that ever hung over Pittsburgh or Los Angeles. (Then came word of their conclusions as to what Mars is like.) The sensitive recording instruments dispatched to that planet have revealed that Mars is almost completely a desert, and that if any life exists there, it must be of a very low order. When will man get it through his head that his choice of a celestial speck to inhabit was a very shrewd one, and that in spite of the mayhem he has committed upon his native Earth, it remains the one hospitable world he is likely to encounter. Let him, then, redouble his efforts to improve it, instead of horsing around beyond its stratosphere.

Space? You can have it. In my estimation, it's for the birds. It was theirs in the first place; let them keep it. Man, God bless him, is a primate, who came down out of the trees only to end up riding bumper to bumper on endless ribbons of concrete, strangling himself in city traffic, cooping himself up in oversized boxes built out of steel, concrete, and glass. He seems at the moment to emulate, above all other forms of animal life, the goldfish. Bankers, once the most secretive of men, now build themselves enormous glass-walled bowls in which their questionable activities are laid open to every passer-by. When at home, Homo sapiens, as he has conceitedly christened himself, delights in burrowing into a huge steel-framed anthill in which, by current building standards, he is privy to whatever noises are most pleasing to his immediate neighbor. This curious compulsion is in full spate from New York to New Delhi. Men once went traveling to remind themselves that not everybody lives alike; now they venture forth to remind themselves that they have never left home.

What can we do about it? Not much, probably, but we might make a try by using words as weapons. Properly employed, they have within them more force than a hundred-megaton bomb.

Suggested Reading
and Reference List

BROWN, IVOR
  A Word in Your Ear and *Just Another Word* (E. P. Dutton)
  I Give You My Word and *Say the Word* (E. P. Dutton. Out of print)
  No Idle Words and *Having the Last Word* (E. P. Dutton. Out of print)
  Words in Season (Rupert Hart-Davis, London)
CAREY, G. V.
  Mind the Stop: A Brief Guide to Punctuation (Cambridge University Press)
DIAMOND, A. S.
  The History and Origin of Language (Philosophical Library)
ERNST, MARGARET S.
  More About Words (Knopf)
EVANS, BERGEN and CORNELIA
  A Dictionary of Contemporary American Usage (Random House)

FOWLER, H. W.
  A Dictionary of Modern English Usage (Oxford)
FUNK, CHARLES EARLE
  Heavens to Betsy! And Other Curious Sayings (Harper)
  Thereby Hangs a Tale: Stories of Curious Word Origins (Harper)
  A Hog On Ice and Other Curious Expressions (Harper)
FUNK, CHARLES EARLE, and CHARLES EARLE, JR.
  Horsefeathers and Other Curious Words (Harper)
FUNK, WILFRED
  Word Origins and Their Romantic Stories (Wilfred Funk)
GREENOUGH, JAMES BRADSTREET, and KITTREDGE, GEORGE LYMAN
  Words and Their Ways in English Speech (Macmillan)
HORWILL, H. W.
  A Dictionary of Modern American Usage (Oxford)
JESPERSON, OTTO
  Growth and Structure of the English Language (Macmillan)
LAIRD, CHARLTON
  The Miracle of Language (World Publishing Co.)
MARTIN, HENRY R.
  Why You Say It (Abingdon Press)
McKNIGHT, GEORGE H.
  Modern English in the Making (Appleton)
MENCKEN, H. L.
  The American Language (Knopf)
  The American Language: Supplement One (Knopf)
  The American Language: Supplement Two (Knopf)
PARTRIDGE, ERIC
  Origins: A Short Etymological Dictionary of Modern English (Macmillan)
  A Dictionary of Slang and Unconventional English (Macmillan)
  Slang Today and Yesterday: A History and a Study (Macmillan)
  Usage and Abusage: A Guide to Good English (Harper, out of print; Hamish Hamilton, London)
  Shakespeare's Bawdry (E. P. Dutton)
  A Charm of Words: Essays and Papers on Language (Macmillan)
  You Have a Point There: A Guide to Punctuation and Its Allies, with an American Chapter by John W. Clark (Hamish Hamilton, London)
  A Dictionary of Clichés (Macmillan)

SKEAT, W. W.
An Etymological Dictionary of the English Language (Oxford)

SMITH, LOGAN PEARSALL
The English Language (Oxford)

STEWART, GEORGE R.
Names on the Land: A Historical Account of Place-Naming in the United States (Houghton Mifflin)

STRUNK, WILLIAM, JR.
The Elements of Style, with revisions, an Introduction and a New Chapter on Writing by E. B. White (Macmillan)

TRENCH, RICHARD CHENEVIX
On the Study of Words and English Past and Present (E. P. Dutton)

VALLINS, G. H.
The Pattern of English (Penguin Books)

WEEKLEY, ERNEST A.
A Concise Etymological Dictionary of Modern English (E. P. Dutton)

WENDELL, BARRETT
English Composition (Charles Scribner's Sons; out of print; Frederick Ungar Publishing Co.)

WENTWORTH, HAROLD and FLEXNER, STUART BERG
Dictionary of American Slang (Thomas Y. Crowell)

WILSON, RICHARD ALBERT
The Miraculous Birth of Language, with a Preface by George Bernard Shaw (Philosophical Library)